POLICY, TECHNOCRACY AND DEVELOPMENT: HUMAN CAPITAL POLICIES IN THE NETHERLANDS AND INDIA

Policy, Technocracy and Development: Human Capital Policies in the Netherlands and India

JAMES WARNER BJÖRKMAN
KULDEEP MATHUR

IDPAD

MANOHAR
2002

First published 2002

ISBN 81-7304-466-X

Published by
Ajay Kumar Jain for
Manohar Publishers & Distributors
4753/23 Ansari Road, Daryaganj
New Delhi 110 002

Typeset by
Kohli Print
Delhi 110 051

Printed at
Rajkamal Electric Press
Delhi 110 033

Contents

Acknowledgements

THE AUTHORS ARE grateful to the Indo-Dutch Programme on Alternatives in Development (IDPAD) and to the Indian Council of Social Science Research for supporting their study (IDPAD-IV 4.3.9) during 1997–2000.

In particular, thanks are due to Dr Reena Barman-Chandra and Dr Srikant Khandewala at ICSSR (New Delhi) and Dr Mark Verhagen at IDPAD (Den Haag), respectively, for facilitating fieldwork and writing in both India and the Netherlands. Without compromising confidentiality, the legion of unnamed interviewees must be thanked for sharing insights into the policy process in both India and the Netherlands. Without their cooperation, this report would not have been possible.

Special thanks are due to the twenty participants of the workshop held in Hyderabad during 6–12 December 1999, who provided a thoroughgoing critique of the draft manuscript as well as additional information. They receive credit for the accomplishments in this report but no blame for any of its shortcomings—the latter being gleefully attributed by the authors to one another.

During the four-year project, many research assistants in Delhi and Den Haag helped to locate (sometimes arcane) data and information, all of whose efforts are much appreciated. In particular, the authors wish to thank Dr J.J. (Youp) van Zorge for his help, not only in field research and preliminary drafting, but also in supervising logistics for the December workshop as well as throughout the project.

The authors also thank two anonymous reviewers for their thoughtful comments and helpful suggestions for revising the final project report into this book.

JAMES WARNER BJÖRKMAN
KULDEEP MATHUR

Chapter 1

Professionals and Public Policy: A Technocratic Hypothesis

ALTHOUGH THE twentieth century has been characterized by major advances in science and technology, few development studies have examined technocratic factors in policy formulation and implementation. Instead, most analysts describe and attempt to explain development plans and results as products of social, political, and (most often) economic factors. While the latter cannot be ignored, analyses of policy choices and applications must examine the role of technocratic factors as well. This study addresses these issues through a comparative analysis of Indian and Dutch policies in primary education and primary health armed towards establishing and sustaining human capital.

Public policy as a field of study began a half-century ago (Lasswell 1951) in an era when the public trusted the government and bureaucrats were largely admired, or at least not despised. Since then, many changes have occurred. Where central direction had once been advocated, devolution is now preferred; democracy and market-based economics have become a global consensus; technology is more dominant, yet questioned as never before; and, perhaps most significantly, the sectors of public, private, non-profit, and citizen endeavour have become less sharply defined and distinct in their missions and goals (Björkman 2000: 22–3). While some things have changed, others remain the same. Lasswell's emphasis on a problem-oriented discipline that takes into account the context of the situation and employs multiple methods of analysis is just as relevant today as it was fifty years ago. This Indo-Dutch study attempts to be similarly holistic through a comparative examination of policy-making processes in the broad field of human capital formation.

At first sight, comparisons between India and the Netherlands may appear to be inapt due to substantial differences in the levels of their socio-economic development. However, similarities between the two exist too. Their systems of government, being deeply democratic and parliamentary, are not very different from each other despite one being structurally a decentralized unitary state and the other a quasi-federal state. Likewise, in both countries technocratization in decision-making has been stimulated by administrative change and overall modernization in recent decades. The pursuit of ambitious developmental goals has served to strengthen the technocratic orientation of public administration. The Netherlands is currently grappling with changes induced by membership in the European Union while India's economic environment has changed since 1991 through the adoption of liberalized economic policies. By varying degrees, the role of the state in each country has been undergoing changes. It would be of considerable practical interest to know how two countries with well-identified differences in their socio-economic development are coping with such changes in order to learn from their experience and to make generalizations about possible patterns of change.

Nomenclature in common usage is almost always imprecise. Terms like expert, professional, and technocrat are frequently interchangeable because their definitional (not to mention behavioural) boundaries overlap. As our purpose in this study is not terminological exactitude but rather an understanding of how public policies are selected and applied, we define technocrats simply as those professionals whose skills and expertize are used within the public arena where they shape the behaviour of others. In terms of standard political science, technocrats are professionals who wield power over others.

As an initial definition, therefore, technocrats in the decision-making process are individuals with high levels of specialist training (particularly in economics and engineering, although medicine perhaps provides the paradigmatic domain) who operate on the principle that most of the problems of society can be solved by scientific and technical means rather than be resolved through politics and social awareness in society (Galjart and Silva 1993). Like professionals, technocrats believe that those who are called upon to solve problems must have specific scientific knowledge to deal with them (Björkman 1982, 1993). Professionalism, of course,

> implies a body of knowledge to be mastered by apprenticeship or formal education, control over recruitment and training to assume mastery of that knowledge, criteria of adequate and inadequate performance,

> of which the professionals themselves are the main judges, and an informal ethos as well as formal rules to govern what professionals regards as technically and ethically correct conduct in relationships to their clients or superiors. (Rudolph and Rudolph 1987: 87)

Specification of technocrats as a strategic group of policy actors in the ordinary sense of the term is, however, problematic. Other categories of policy actors are more obvious. Politicians are those who are elected (or aspire to be elected, or selected by other means) to decision-making roles—and, by extended implication in popular votes, provide legitimation for government decisions. And bureaucrats or civil servants are those who, recruited and trained along generalist lines, follow administrative careers in public service organizations. While technocrats as defined above can certainly engage in both political and bureaucratic roles, we argue that their allegiance to professional norms of behaviour transcends both political and bureaucratic loyalties. The problem of identification is exacerbated by the fact that technocrats tend to eschew the label because to be called a technocrat often implies pejorative connotations as well. Indeed, in our populist democratic era, governments avoid recognizing or acknowledging the increasing technocratization of decision-making because of its elitist implications.

These factors (difficulty of identification and negative connotations) may largely explain why the subject has not previously been addressed by scholars of development and change. In fact, in a type of self-limiting reiteration, scholars *per se* are quintessential examples of technocrats—and consequently they not only hesitate to draw attention to their own roles and powers but also find it difficult to be self-critical and auto-analytic. As perhaps understandably automatic compensation, scholars/analysts see themselves as autonomous agents who are not bound by group interests. In old-fashioned Marxist terms, they sometimes label themselves as the intelligentsia and claim to be a 'stratum' rather than a 'class'. Hopefully, however, contemporary empirical rigour can overcome these self-serving devices.

An examination of the social and political processes in various countries of both the North and the South reveals that intellectuals and scholars have been much more than dispassionate analysts who are dedicated to describing activities in other levels of society. In many cases, they can be identified as key actors in the profound social and political changes that have swept the world during the past half-century. One can find technocrats at the side of both the power-holders and their challengers. As architects and engineers of development, technocrats have provided political leaders the ideological, institutional, and economic models needed to run their countries. And, of course, some technocrats supply the dissident intellectuals who often play a strategic role in organizing oppositional forces against dictatorships of all kinds. In short, although collectively labelled, the category of technocrats merits systematic attention and analysis.

There are crude harbingers of the emergence—and then the increasing activity—of technocrats in a political system. Simple measures of initial literacy, followed by specialized training, provide the context for subsequent political activity. Social modernization and the expansion of educational opportunities are important factors in any explanation for the rise of technocracy. Clearly, technocratic hegemony depends on the presence of a significant number of technocrats, a condition which becomes possible only if there is a relatively well-developed, complex system of higher education. Therefore, one may hypothesize that *technocratization of decision-making correlates significantly with the emergence of a large, important middle-class* and, by extension, that *technocratization deepens or becomes more pervasive with increasing wealth and well-being.*

In terms of the current comparative study, this phenomenon of technocratization in decision-making has been stimulated by administrative and overall modernization in recent decades. Where rationality is the dominant theme for allocation of resources, technocracy not only becomes more important but also reinforces itself. In both the era of master planning and the era of globalized liberalism, ambitious developmental goals pursued by many governments have served to strengthen the technocratic orientation of public administration in the context of complex societies. This observation is as true for the Netherlands as it is for India, since the former is increasingly enmeshed in changes and growth induced by membership in the European Union while the latter is experiencing both economic expansion with a burgeoning middle-class and economic immiseration of a proliferating underclass. While comparisons of the systems in the two countries may initially appear somewhat stretched or forced, there are valid grounds on which to examine their differences as well as their similarities.

As preliminary evidence of technocratization, the process was set in motion by the expansion of the state apparatus (particularly the bureaucracy in the civil service and public sector undertakings), the nationalization of many industrial sectors as well as natural resources, the application (and, often, legal avoidance or negation) of land reforms, and the initiation (if incomplete implementation) of huge social programmes. The last mentioned policy area is our point of entry to trace the development of such technocratization, its dynamics, and its effects.

The increasing complexity and urgency of macroeconomic problems have strengthened the position of highly qualified individuals at the top levels within government circles (Mathur and Björkman 1994). Economic and financial crises during the 1970s and 1980s forced many countries to accept stabilization programmes and structural adjustment programmes formulated by international financial institutions (most notably the World Bank and the International Monetary Fund). These crises occurred throughout the world (including within some members of the Organization for Economic Cooperation and Development), but particularly in less developed countries (LDCs) where local economists and fiscal experts effectively consolidated their strategic positions within the ruling elites. This sector has been modestly well-reported because, in contrast to traditional intellectuals, technocratic specialists in macroeconomics as well as fiscal and monetary policies were prepared to deal with issues which received priority at top governmental levels—for example, foreign debt, inflation, balance of payments, trade deficits, budget deficits, unemployment, and the general search for foreign loans as well as new markets.

Interestingly, the increasingly evident importance of economic technocrats within the leading groups in many countries has not (at least yet) led to the formulation of a theoretical interpretation that explains this phenomenon nor accounts for its relative weight in different countries. The most suggestive theory thus far harkens back to the power of professionals in the traditional arenas of law, medicine, and even theology. A profession contains both intellectuals and technocrats (that is, both producers as well as users of ideas/knowledge), although the behaviour of professionals is weighted toward technocratic rather than intellectual functions because the former are explicitly characterized as rule by technique (the direct translation of technocracy). While intellectual functions may 'rule' within a profession where degrees of knowledge serve to rank-order positions of status, the rule that is projected outside the circle of professionals is through application of techniques that dominate the uninitiated.

The members of a profession—or at least its preponderant majority—have 'common ways of perceiving and structuring problems and of attacking and solving them; . . . are likely to share their views of the world and of the place of their profession in it; [and] . . . are likely also to share a common, and more or less unique, bundle of techniques, skills, knowledge and vocabulary' (Mosher 1978: 147). These shared attributes are generated and sustained by self-recruitment, by educational training, and by socialization on the job within a given organization or series of organizations. A profession thus dominates the division of labour within its ecological niche (Friedson 1985: 13). But professionalism as a core of identity requires self-conscious identification. When applied by analysts, the label is often only an analytic category. To become the basis for identification and then action, professionalism must be an attribute perceived, experienced, and consciously felt by the members of the group. Therefore, the greater the fuzziness of knowledge or the more diffuse and ambiguous are its boundaries, the lower the degree of psychological coherence among the members of a socalled profession.

Professional education is particularly important because the pressure of university academics has generated increasingly theoretical and research-oriented knowledge as well as increasingly fragmented sub-specializations. It has been observed that such highly specialized university training provides little that is useful to effective practice by professionals, but corrective action takes place on-the-job as freshly-minted apprentices 'unlearn' and re-adapt their knowledge. Nonetheless, most professions continue to stress their links to specialized higher education while pressures continue to make educational requisites ever higher and more specialized. Such links are still needed to justify a profession's claim to exclusivity, elite status, autonomy and self-governance (Björkman 1982).

Professionals—or, better still, the technocrats who believe in the rectitude and relevance of specialized knowledge—influence the course of governmental action and policy implementation individually or in concert with others. The principal channels (which are not mutually exclusive) through they do so are those of:

- Election or, more usually, appointment of professionals to high office;
- Effective control, often a near-monopoly, of significant managerial positions of administrative agencies by individual professions—positions that need not be at the pinnacle of an agency's organization chart, but must at least occupy its secondary and tertiary levels;
- Pressures brought to bear on political executives and/or legislative bodies by indirect means—that is, by professional associations, lobbying by mobilized experts, the media, publication of research results, etc.; and
- Networks of professional ties ('old-boy' links, schools, associations) across the boundaries of separate governmental agencies and organizations.

Drawing on a series of symposia in the *Public Administration Review*, Mosher (1978: 146) classified a dozen professions in the US according to the relative importance of these channels of influence. He concluded that of these, 'the control of a specialized professional agency is the most frequent, and probably most important, channel of professional influence'.

A significant channel of influence of experts on government emerges through their membership on committees that governments appoint to obtain advise about specific issues. As social complexities have increased, governments have moved away from their own in-house expertise of bureaucrats and technocrats and looked instead to external experts for alternative policy advice. Experts are not appointed to formal government posts nor do they represent their professional organizations when they join committees. They usually act as individual experts and participate with others in formulating advice. Because acting as a group tends to iron out individual biases and create broad agreement, advice by a committee becomes more formidable and transparent than if it had been rendered by a single expert. This procedure facilitates accountability and offers opportunities for public discussion and debate on technical matters, but it also makes it more complex to trace the roles of experts and technocrats in the policy process.

While important for the implementation of complex policies, professionals and technocrats cannot be controlled through democratic accountability systems. Majority voting does not and cannot direct expertise because the former is too crude, too fickle, and sometimes quite wrong in terms of the canons of received scientific opinion. Of course, majority voting can restrict professionals from practising altogether by banning their activities or even their very existence; and majoritarian law can levy penalties and sanctions that set broad parameters of conscionable conduct by professionals. But expertise is not subject to validation (or disproof/rejection/falsification) by majority voting.

Economic accountability would seem a more likely method to control professionals, at least if a balanced market for exchanges could exist. But, given the specialized knowledge and expertize on which a profession is based, the relationship between providers and consumers is inherently imbalanced. With few exceptions, the exchange relationship is asymmetrical; and it tends toward monopoly control over passive recipients. This asymmetry is particularly acute in the health sector where conditions of disease, illness, and/or death elevate the status of providers while simultaneously reducing the patients to a state of dependency. This asymmetry is also prevalent in the educational realm, which is characterized by differentials between the teachers and the taught. The claims of knowledge and expertise produce a self-fulfilling prophecy.

Although the boundaries between categories like technocrats, bureaucrats, academics, professionals, and experts are vague and imprecise (and indeed can be crossed by single individuals), some conceptual order can be established among them. In all cases, power (the ability to make others do [or not do] what they do not [or do] want to do) is being wielded—particularly power based on respect for knowledge, shared norms, 'scientific' status, or at least persuasion. However, in the chronological development process, not only may the bases of this technocratic power change (for example, from religion to ideology to science), but also the occupations in which people earn a living, or exert their influence, may change in number and configuration. In the historical flow of human capital policies over time, regularities may well appear. Likewise, particular periods in one or another country may reveal that some ideas (or sets or systems of ideas) have greater or lesser influence than other systems of ideas.

The pattern of the influence of ideas may indicate the reasons for their relative popularity, and the extent to which one set of arguments is protected against counter-arguments. Above all, no matter how worthy or 'scientific' such ideas and ideals may be, studies will reveal the extent to which professionals and technocrats (or select sets among them) act as interest groups at certain times. This study focuses attention on the role of experts and technocrats as members of committees giving policy advice to governments. There are experts who hold government office, but they are not our primary concern.

In order to delimit the research, this study restricts its investigations to the committee processes of rendering policy advice. Because individual experts work with others, our research question has asked how collective recommendations are derived. Therefore, attention has been largely focused on policy processes and not on the substantive issues of policy *per se*. Apart from using sources of secondary data, interviews were conducted during the course of the study with a significant number of bureaucrats and professionals who had served on advisory committees in the Netherlands and India. Some of these respondents attended a seminar workshop in December 1999 in Hyderabad (India) where the initial findings of the study were presented for preliminary discussion. This final report has benefited greatly from the trenchant criticisms and helpful suggestions as well as additional information and insights provided by participants in the Hyderabad workshop.

Chapter 2

Trends in the Netherlands

From Liberal State through Pillarized State to Steering State

Until the nineteenth century, Dutch governments rarely provided educational and health care services (Israel 1998). Ordinary citizens, either individually or in associations, undertook those tasks that are now widely accepted as public obligations. Government was expected only to create the necessary conditions under which private initiatives could operate. Over time, however, government was increasingly compelled to regulate standards as well as to ensure a wider coverage of services. Private awareness thus preceded government involvement in the Netherlands, as it had elsewhere in Europe (Heclo 1970).

At the same time, Dutch society was fragmented and organized along the lines of four social groups or 'pillars' within familiar religious/secular cleavages: Roman Catholic, Protestant, *laissez-faire* Liberal, and Socialist Labour. When state intervention began to appear, it not only respected these social demarcations but also augmented their importance, thereby contributing to the establishment of a 'pillarized' society during the first half of the twentieth century. The gradual transition from a liberal state to a pillarized state was facilitated by the concept of subsidization wherein pillarized organizations, although private in nature, were incorporated into the public domain by subsidies. The public domain thus came to display a markedly segmented character.

A so-called 'consociational democracy' held this fragmented society together. While each pillar was distinct and self-sufficient at its base, their elites cooperated at the top. Lijphart (1984) dates the origin of consociational democracy in the 1913–17 period. Prior to that disagreements on several major (primarily educational and social) issues had fuelled hostility among the groups. The 1917 'Pacification' pact initiated a period of elite cooperation that kept the groupings together despite their fractious tendencies.

However, there were limits to cooperation. In the pillarized society, cleavages among the four main social groupings were such that the Central government could handle only a few issues (and usually only in a procedural way), thus leaving as much substantive decision-making as possible to the pillars themselves. Each pillar organized its own socio-economic and private life. It created its own welfare organizations (for income, health, housing, education), industrial corporations, trade unions, services, banks, and so forth (van Schendelen 1987: 65). Roman Catholics initiated the doctrine of 'subsidiarity' wherein the state should only do what (Roman Catholic) society could not do by itself. Therefore, the state should not interfere with the personal, domestic, church and scientific life of its citizens. Dutch Protestants called this arrangement 'sovereignty in one's own circle' (*sovereiniteit in eigen kring*). This particular mode of organization had important consequences for Dutch government and politics. The pillarized society led to the emergence of Dutch corporatism, a fragmented bureaucratic apparatus, depoliticized cabinets, and an increasing role for experts in policy-making.

Structural Pluralism, Well-being, and Dutch Corporatism

The concept of corporatism describes an empirical relationship between interest groups and government that is based on an exchange (of influence for support) and on cooperation rather than competition. The Dutch usage of the concept entails that socio-economic decision-making is done within the branches of production and coordinated in a body that replaces parliament (van Holthoon 1988: 71). Because both government and private organizations were active in a wide array of public sectors (with financing and regulatory roles mainly for government and a managerial role for the private institutions), there were perceived needs for a division of power and responsibilities as well as a place where government and interest groups could meet.

Over the years the Dutch government, therefore, created a bewildering variety of advisory boards, tripartite councils, and parastatal organizations. The most illustrative examples are the post-war public law organizations for economic activity (*Publieksrechtelijke Bedrijfs Organisaties*, PBO) that were created in order to allow government to transfer some of its responsibilities to independent regulatory commissions, in which representatives of workers and employers together with government appointees regulate their particular sector of the economy. In these socio-economic regulatory commissions, the pillarized interest groups were heavily represented.

The most important PBO is the Socio-Economic Council (SER) which is comprised of representatives of employer organizations, trade unions, and Crown members. Crown members are appointed by the Central government, but can act independently from it. Crown members include the Governor of the Dutch National Bank, the Director of the Central Planning Bureau, and some university professors in economics. As experts these Crown members are expected to have a moderating effect on the debate between the clashing interest groups of employers and trade unions.

Based on consociational democracy and adherence to the subsidiarity principle, a solution for the fragmentation of Dutch society was found in the establishment of a corporatist state organization. During the 1960s, however, depillarization produced more rather than less fragmentation. It broke down the easily recognizable homogeneous segments into numerous smaller groups without replacing the former intrapillar integrating mechanisms with some functional equivalent (Andeweg and Irwin 1993: 229). These smaller fragments benefited from the already existing functional decentralization and replaced the 'old' pillarized organizations in the decision-making process. This new form of collaboration between the state and several cohesive interest groups is referred to as neocorporatism. Neo-corporatism further strengthens the functional decentralization and subsequent sectorization of policy-making, which, in turn, leads to specialization and more influence for technocratic experts.

Fragmentation of Dutch Bureaucracy

Decentralization to largely autonomous 'policy sectors'—each composed of interest groups, advisory boards, (sections of) a government department, and specialized committees in parliament—caused the fragmentation of the Dutch bureaucracy. Neo-corporatist networks surrounding each department reinforce departmental autonomy. Each department is largely autonomous and sets its own entrance standards, which generally require training or expertise in a specific policy area. Once appointed to a specific department, a civil servant tends to spend his/her entire career within the confines of that department, often within a single directorate.

The relationship between government and administration is not, of course, merely a question of economic efficiency. As with all other societal institutions, administrative agencies are subject to a struggle of social forces that may differ from one policy field to another. It is not easy to discover patterns, not even in a single country. But the Netherlands has often been characterized as a struggle between étatists and corporatists as well as between those who prefer a strong central government and those who advocate strong local government instead. Another complicating factor is the cleavage between social political groups such as Catholics, Protestants, Social Democrats, and Liberal Conservatives. Over the years, a number of varied coalitions have been formed that have produced an extremely complex and kaleidoscopic pattern of allocation mechanisms. The government apparatus has been used by all kinds of interest groups to promote not the general interest but their own ends. Such self-interested networks are rarely blatant but subtlety implicated in the processes of recruitment and training being decentralized by ministries (Aquina and Bekke 1993: 159–70).

Any attempt to increase the mobility of civil servants is frustrated by the high degree of specialization. This technocratic specialization is not offset by political appointments because these rarely occur. In order not to offend any minority, decisions are often based on technical rather than ideological motives, which explains why civil servants must be highly specialized in a particular policy field rather than in more general managerial skills. The consequences of such specialization are the emergence of distinct departmental cultures and structures, increasing fragmentation, and limited inter-departmental mobility.

Depoliticized Cabinets and Non-decision-making

The Dutch traits of consensus-seeking and inclination to non-decision-making are known internationally. These traits derive from the pillarized history of the Netherlands in which a delicate balance had to be found among the four population groupings. Avoidance of decision-making takes three frequently practised forms: postponement of decisions, dilution of political disputes by technical arguments (depoliticization), and removal of responsibility from the government. The establishment of temporary expert committees (preferably composed proportionally) to study a problem is a device that combines these three tactics with an almost inevitable result, as the jargon has it, of 'putting hot potatoes in the refrigerator' (Andeweg and Irwin 1993: 38).

Although less numerous and less influential than before, standing external expert committees remain important collections of experts. Government is surrounded by forecasting and fact-finding agencies like the Central Bureau of Statistics (CBS), the Central Planning Bureau (CPB) for economic forecasting, the Town and Country Planning Agency (RPD), the Scientific Council for Government Policy (WRR), and the Social and Cultural Planning Bureau (SCP). And it is not only the government that makes use of these agencies; their reports are customarily published and play an important role in public debate. Permanent external advisory councils (three-quarters of whose members are recruited from organized interests) form an important avenue through which technocrats can exert influence. Most advisory councils have their own expert staff. For example, there are five major advisory councils on public health; combined they employ more experts in their secretariats than the government's own Directorate of Public Health.

At least until the 1960s, technocratization extended into the cabinet itself. Selection criteria for ministers were often more technocratic rather than political, so that there was a banker or economist as the finance minister, a lawyer as the minister for justice, a farmer as the agriculture minister, etc. The non-political nature of civil service recruitment added to the technocratic nature of cabinets. Unlike the spoils system or *cabinet ministériel* that exists in France, Belgium, and Italy, the notable absence of departmental political advisers contributes to the emphasis of a Dutch minister's departmental rather than political role. Ministers are briefed on cabinet papers by their department officials, and these departmental briefings are based on rather narrow interpretations of the department's interest rather than on partisan politics.

Given that the Dutch governments have mostly been coalitions of political parties, the apolitical and technical nature of Dutch cabinets is all the more surprising. The explanation lies in the delicate balance among the four major components of a fragmented society and the consociational democratic solution. If stable government was threatened by subcultural strife, the cabinet had to remain detached from daily political squabbles and focus instead on technical matters (Andeweg and Irwin 1993: 128).

Since 1967 (the apparent beginning of the end of pillarization) the political nature of the cabinet has increased. But, despite the growing influence of the political parties on the cabinet, it remains safe to say—as did former Prime Minister Drees in 1965—that functional [that is, departmental] conflicts tend to be more important than political conflicts. Even in the 1995–2001 'purple coalition', Dutch ministers still tend to be specialists: the present minister of health is a former medical doctor while the present minister of finance is a former banker.

However fragmented the Dutch society may be, there is an underlying consensus that considerably constrains the scope of political conflict. Consensus is actively sought through consultation and depoliticization, for both of which activities the contribution of professional experts is crucial.

> The role of experts goes beyond keeping the debate between opposing parties or interest groups honest. They are often instrumental in forging a consensus where none previously existed, as technocratic findings seem to take precedence over ideological values. Indeed, without this respect for experts, depoliticization could not have become such an important device in the politics of accommodation'. (Andeweg and Irwin 1993: 232)

Independent experts are crucial in neo-corporatist policy-making because they provide a common framework and acceptable data, which are evidence of a pervasive ideology of social partnership. This ideology incorporates a continuous reaffirmation of political differences with political cooperation.

Chapter 3

Trends in India

Socio-Political Context

Given its size and heterogeneity, India is not an easy country to govern. Many of its component states are larger in both area and population than several other sovereign nations. A federal system of government exists in India but, in contrast to the United States which has a population of about 270 million divided among 50 states, India's population of 1 billion is distributed unequally across 35 states and union territories. The border areas of north-east and north-west India continue to be politically troubled areas. For this reason the twin issues of national unity and integrity have dominated the policy concerns of the Central government since Independence in 1947. A consequence of such thinking has been hesitant decentralization and the reluctant opening of decision-making processes to wider sources of consultation and advice.

At the time that India adopted a democratic parliamentary system of government with universal adult franchise over half its population was classified as living below the poverty line and the literacy rate was around 35 per cent. Much of the effort since then has been directed towards empowering the people to exercise their franchise effectively by raising literacy rates and by reducing poverty levels. The discourse on democracy has centred around the core liberal concepts of individual rights, freedom, and equal opportunity. Given these ideals, desperate accounts are often heard about how democracy is not functioning well in the Indian context. The decline in the quality of public life and the state's incapacity to meet the growing demands of the people are attributed to the pathology of the democratic political system.

Indeed, India does face a paradox. Social conflicts have been rising, the economy has been passing through difficult periods, and democratic institutions are continuously put under strain in trying to stem the tide of protest and violence in the country. Democracy, on the other hand, seems to have deepened and widened its reach (Lijphart 1996). The proportion of socially and economically deprived people casting their vote in the electoral ballot has risen in recent years.

The higher level of turbulence in the recent electoral outcomes can be attributed the expansion of the participatory base of electoral democracy during the 1990s. Today the odds that a socially and economically deprived person will vote are much higher than when the country started on its path of democratic governance (Yadav 1999).

This democratic experience has severely strained the system of governance, particularly after the democratic participatory upsurge in the last two decades. The difficulties have been compounded by the pattern of economic development in the country. While the goals of economic growth and removal of poverty have continued to dominate the development discourse, the actual outcome of policies has been far from ideal. Population growth has continued to hover around 2–2.5 per cent per year and, because the rate of per capita income growth has been slightly lower than the population growth rate, there has been little impact on poverty levels. Literacy rates have risen but almost half the population remains unable to read and write. While economic development has taken place, it is also highly skewed. Some regions and states have done rather well but several states with the largest populations have lagged considerably behind. The dilemma of increased political participation within a system of restrictive economic benefits is the major challenge that policy-makers face as India enters a new millennium.

In socio-religious terms, India is characterized by religious

TABLE 3.1: DECENNIAL INDICATORS OF HUMAN DEVELOPMENT IN INDIA SINCE INDEPENDENCE

Year	*Life expectancy*	*Literacy rate*	*Birth rate*	*Death rate*	*Infant mortality*
1951	32.1	18.3	39.9	27.4	146
1961	41.3	28.3	41.7	22.8	146
1971	45.6	34.5	36.9	14.9	129
1981	50.4	43.6	33.9	12.5	110
1991	59.4	52.2	29.5	9.5	80

pluralism although the vast majority of Indians are Hindus—less than a fifth (about 17 per cent) of the population belong to other religions. Before as well as after Independence, religion has been an effective wellspring of political mobilization. The Indian Constitution of 1950 carried forward the legacy of the freedom struggle, dominated by the Congress party, when it enshrined the principles of secularism and respect for all religions. Nonetheless, the Hindu nationalists hotly debate these principles while the minorities demand the just implementation of constitutional liberties and safeguards.

Jawaharlal Nehru had argued that there was no social truth in the communal definition of the interests of the people. He further stated that if attention was paid towards the vital problems facing the country—that is, the problem of Independence and of elimination of poverty and unemployment—there is no difference between the Muslim, Hindu, Sikh, or Christian masses in the country. The British policy of divide-and-rule was also seen as an instrument of dividing the people on communal lines. Hence, Independence was expected to provide the setting of a political discourse that would be based not on religion but on constitutional arrangements and alternative means of solving socio-economic problems. Such expectations have been belied as Hindu nationalism has taken a fundamentalist form that attacks the secular provisions of the Constitution as evidence of weakness and as appeasement of the minorities. Assertive Hinduism has led to the formation of several socio-cultural organizations propagating a single culture and single identity for all those who live in India. The political formation based on this ideology is the Bharatiya Janata Party (BJP), which has in recent years gained respectability by coming to power at the federal level as well as in a few of the constituent states.

For several decades, the politics of language has been dormant. Politics has instead been dominated by Hindu assertions of 'one religion, one nation' and countered by the politics of caste identity and demand on state resources by the Dalits, other backward castes, and all other religions. While India's social diversities are not easy to recount, some stand out prominently. These have also shaped the performance of the political and administrative system. Virtually all Hindus can be differentiated from one another by caste. Even non-Hindu communities like Muslims and Christians, who are doctrinally committed to absolute equality of all individuals, identify themselves by caste. One is born into a caste and can renounce it but rarely can one join a caste other than that of his or her parents. There is a broad fourfold division among castes but what affects everyday life is a myriad of *jatis* or endogamous communities into which these castes are subdivided. These *jatis* shape social identities and determine social behaviour.

There are also a large number of people outside these *jatis* who are considered outcastes or untouchables. Traditionally, they have performed the most menial of tasks like scavenging, etc., and have remained the poorest of all. Approximately 20 per cent of India's population are in this category, which outnumbers the followers of all the minority religions combined. Mahatma Gandhi tried to bring them into the mainstream by renaming them Harijans or the Children of God, and by calling for social reform. But the most famous leader of the outcastes and untouchables, Dr B.R. Ambedkar, contested this process by arguing that such assimilation was not possible because of the way the Hindu society was structured. Ambedkar therefore advocated a separate identity for all untouchables by calling them Dalits or the oppressed. This radical reformist strand ultimately led the Ambedkarites to renounce Hinduism altogether and to embrace Buddhism instead. This cleavage has continued to create dissension in India's post-Independence society and polity.

The caste system has divided Indian society not only socially but also economically. Almost by definition, the upper castes have been part of the ruling classes in the country. They have taken advantage of all state resources and, even after Independence, have continued to remain socially and economically powerful. But this monopoly of power has not remained entirely stable. The right to equality has been enshrined in the Constitution while decision-rules based on majoritarian democracy recognize the principle of 'one man, one vote'. The Constitution also includes specific measures to help the lower and backward castes uplift themselves through policies that provided them reservations in government jobs and in educational institutions. The post-Independence period has been a struggle to democratize the society through the provisions laid down in the Constitution. Caste identities and issues of caste representation became politically significant, and political parties articulating such interests have periodically cropped up. As caste considerations have started playing a crucial role in determining policies, it has become important to assess policies on the basis of their impact on the deprived castes.

The language landscape has even greater diversities. The Constitution has listed 16 officially recognized languages and made Hindi the official language of the federal government. Initially, English was expected to be phased out by 1965, fifteen years after the Constitution had been promulgated. However, the Official Languages Act of 1963 conceded indefinite use of English in addition to Hindi, and assured the non-Hindi speaking states that Hindi would not be imposed on them against their will. Hindi and the regional languages were to be promoted through a three-language formula in education, which expected that English, Hindi and the local vernacular (or mother tongue) would simultaneously be taught at the school level. The issue of the appropriate medium of instruction at the primary level leads to political debates even now. Nevertheless, employment opportunities continue to be English oriented, so that English has grown phenomenally and continues to remain the source of jobs and power. However, because English is spoken by only a small percentage of the total population, the majority of Indians regard it more as a symbol of dominance and power than as a window to knowledge and the outside world.

Two kinds of interconnected language struggles have appeared in the post-Independence period. One, coupled with attempts to promote Hindi and regional languages, is directed against English. The other is the use of regional languages as a source of identity and culture. In 1956 the patchwork of princely states and colonial presidencies was reorganized on a linguistic basis, but thereafter no further division of states has been demanded on the basis of language. However, English continues to gain in strength as more and more parents opt for the private educational system that imparts instruction in English. The catch is that English medium education is expensive and hence restricted to those who can pay for it. For the vast majority of pupils who attend the government schools, education continues to be provided in Hindi or one of the regional languages. English thus plays an important role in creating as well as reinforcing social divisions of privilege. Yet at the same time, it is also a symbol of entry into the middle class.

From Colonial State through Dominant-Party State to Coalitional State

India's political formations have significantly changed during the past half-century. The All-India Congress, which had organized the successful independence movement, has been India's leading political party, winning in seven of the eight general elections held by the time it celebrated its centenary in 1985. The Congress then lost in the 1989 general elections, returned to power in 1991, but lost again in the subsequent general elections of 1996 and 1998. The non-Congress coalitions that have led the Government of India have been shaky and none of them have been able to complete a full five-year term of office. In the general elections of September–October 1999, the Congress again lost badly as the electorate returned to power an unwieldy but strengthened 22-party alliance led by the BJP. For the first time since 1970, a government has been returned to power—and, for the first time ever, a coalition has been re-elected.

The changing fortunes of the Congress party have profoundly influenced Indian politics and government and have shaped the emergence of other parties. As a party spearheading the national movement to get rid of the colonial rule, the Congress party had been an umbrella party trying to put together all the diverse interests with a common nationalist goal of ousting the imperial power. It succeeded in doing so by creating an elaborate democratic organizational structure, which incorporated these diverse interests. Because of this heterogeneity of interests being united for a nationalist purpose, Mahatma Gandhi saw the Congress as a movement rather than a party and advocated its dissolution once independence had been achieved. But his major lieutenants, Jawaharlal Nehru and Vallabhbhai Patel, disagreed on this, as did most other Congress leaders. Consequently, although some committed Gandhians resigned their memberships and left the party, the Congress party continued its political activities and contested the 1951 general elections. However, its concern to maintain itself as a consensus party containing all kinds of caste, community, or regional interests continued to dominate its policies of mobilization. Over the years it emerged as a centrist 'catch-all' party without a cadre and without a strong ideological base.

The process of consensus building was the most important characteristic of the party. Nehru's personal domination of the party and the government did not overly constrain inner party democracy. Internal democracy was maintained at least for two reasons. First, Nehru took his role of implanting parliamentary and democratic institutions into India rather seriously. Secondly, his colleagues—both in government and party—were those with whom he had personal relationships from the days of the freedom struggle when they were his companions in the British jails. They could advise him candidly without threatening his leadership. Thus dissent was expressed openly and accepted in that spirit. The organizational structure of the party was also such that it allowed for elections at every level from the local base upwards, with the parliamentary and organizational wings working together.

Its organizational structure allowed the party to transform itself from a national movement into a party of governance. It also helped in creating a conciliatory machinery within the party at various levels that prevented local or regional conflicts from becoming issues of national importance. This particular characteristic prevented individual or group interests from dominating national interests until at least the early 1970s and also discouraged individuals and groups from leaving the party to pursue their particularistic goals. The consequence of the continuation of such a party was that in a multi-party system, where free competition among parties occurred, a single party—the All-India Congress—dominated. For this reason, Kothari (1964) and Morris-Jones (1978) characterized India as a 'one party dominant system'. Manor (1988) points out that the management of resources—at which many in the Congress excelled—was essential to achieve reconciliation, to mediate in factional disputes, and to influence political decisions at state and district levels. Manor further described the Congress party as a giant system of 'transactional linkages', a mechanism for the distribution of spoils in return for political support and organizational loyalty. The main integrating ideas were opportunism, self-aggrandizement, the impulse to enter into patron–client relationships, and to forge deals. As a consequence the role of the party in policy-making gradually diminished while its place as an integrating mechanism in society came to be strengthened.

After Nehru's death in 1964, the conciliatory machinery of the party came under strain for various reasons. Apart from the absence Nehru's charisma that had held the party together, state resources began to dwindle and the rate of public investment began to decline. It was not possible to maintain a mechanism wherein such resources could be exchanged for political support and organizational loyalty. Up to the 1960s, much of the success of the Congress party has been attributed by observers to its ability to forge widespread patronage networks, which provided a crucial linkage between local demands and central responses, which helped to solve a variety of power conflicts (Weiner 1967; Kothari 1975). Gradually, however, these links were destroyed. No elections were held within the party after 1972 as Indira Gandhi began appointing persons to both party and governmental positions based on their personal loyalty to her rather than for their ability to articulate grassroot demands. These appointees did not have the capacity to influence local behaviour nor could they mediate in social and political conflicts. As a result Congress lost its pre-eminent role in the Indian political system. During the 1985 centenary celebrations, Rajiv Gandhi referred to this decline when he said that Congress had become a party of brokers 'who dispense patronage to convert a mass movement into a feudal oligarchy' (Björkman and Mathur 1996: 29).

Unlike its previous incarnation, the party from the 1970s onwards became a centralized organization owing loyalty to a single leader. It lost touch with real issues and was interested in government only so long as the flow of patronage continued. Loyalty to a leader was also based on the ability to ensure this flow. The result was that the party fell prey to internal bickering and factional fights that were more personal than policy related.

The decline of the Congress party coincided with the rise of sectarian interests on the national scene. Parties with regional, caste and community interests emerged, and alliances among these parties formed coalition governments in 1989, 1996 and 1998. The very nature of these alliances has meant that many contradictory interests have had, to be carried together and each alliance has disintegrated due to incompatible expectations. While centralizing tendencies have led to the dismemberment of the Congress party, the other parties by the very nature of their origin exhibit similar disintegrating tendencies. The Congress party itself has become reduced to one among many in contrast to the hegemonic position it had earlier occupied in the political system. While coalitions, too, present a picture of instability.

Coherent public policies have not emerged from these governments because their existence is based on a short-term strategy to share political power. Yet it appears that the coalitions tend to follow a middle path. The situation appears to differ little from that prevailing during the rule of the Congress governments themselves. The all-embracing character of the Congress party meant that consensus became the dominant mode of determining policies because the Congress party placed much higher emphasis on its role as an integrating mechanism in society. For different reasons this emphasis is true also for the coalitions whose affiliating parties are more interested in pursuing their own interests rather than forging a national policy. What emerges as national policy is a product of bargaining over the fulfilment of their own interests. There is little possibility of radical policies emerging from such coalitions. To date, political parties that have joined the coalitions have not insisted on a minimal level of achievement for a joint manifesto, and hence little monitoring of the implementation occurs. Therefore, whether there are Congress or coalitional governments, concerns about manifestos and their implementation are never high on the political agenda.

Two other characteristics of the Indian governmental system influence political behaviour. One is that India has a federal system of government, which, however, has are strong centralizing tendencies. For one, all residuary powers fall within the purview of the Centre. Secondly, the Centre holds the purse strings and has powers to discipline the states both in its financial as well as executive functions. The result is that states are dependent on the Centre and serve as its executive arm. Thus, much of the educational policy or health policy is decided at the Central level but is implemented by the states. In many cases, even this arrangement is given a go-by when the Centre chooses to install its own implementing agency at the field level. The process of planning has given further strength to the supremacy of the Central government. An integral part of the struggle by the regional parties coming to power in the states after the decline of the Congress has been the demand for greater autonomy in local areas of concern.

One aspect of this demand has been to create strong local level democratic institutions of governance. During the 1950s when centralized planning held sway, concern for local level participation for mobilizing support for central plans was expressed through the creation of Panchayati Raj institutions. From the village upward to the district level, a system of democratically elected local government was created. It was inaugurated with fanfare in 1959 but went into rapid decline within a few years. The reasons for this were many but infrequent elections, conflict with local bureaucracy, and lack of finance were among the more prominent factors (Björkman and Chaturvedi 1994). Thus, a centralized bureaucracy continued to manage and implement programmes that were squarely in the arenas of local concern. Local government once again became an issue in the late 1970s because of the rise of agrarian classes as a political force.

Efforts to revitalize the Panchayati Raj institutions began during the period of Rajiv Gandhi's prime ministership (1984–9) and finally fructified when the Congress party came back to power in 1991. In 1993, constitutional amendments made this revitalization possible by giving considerable autonomy to Panchayati Raj institutions that were established at district and lower levels. Local primary schools and health centres are sought to be put under people's control through these institutions. Such decentralization has generated opposition not only from political leaders but also the functionaries of these agencies due to the fear of constant accountability.

The Indian bureaucracy provides another source of impediment to the decentralization and strengthening of local democratic institutions. The Indian administrative system carries strong vestiges of the past and members of the Indian Administrative Service (IAS), successor to the British Indian Civil Service, hold critical positions from the district level up to the state and central secretariat. There is a strong chain of command and as a single group the IAS is responsible for formulating and implementing all crucial decisions. The educational and health hierarchies are subservient to it and have only an advisory role. This characteristic has led to a situation where expertise is only on tap and cannot determine policies unless upheld by the IAS.

Pluralism, Poverty, and the Indian Middle Class

The leadership of the national movement was comprised largely of urban professionals and intellectuals who identified the future of the country with the developments in the West, particularly the potential of science and technology to transform societies. Nehru was fascinated by developments in Soviet Russia and impressed by the achievements made possible by planning and the rational use of resources. He visualized India quickly attaining the levels of economic development achieved by the Western nations and simultaneously eliminating poverty. Mahatma Gandhi's views were in stark contrast because he did not want India to follow the path of the industrialized West, whether capitalist or communist. For him development was a moral issue that took into account all facets of individual living. To remove poverty he wanted all individuals, and likewise villages, to be self-reliant. The resources to be used were homegrown. Therefore, Gandhi favoured small-scale cottage industries as a means of bringing prosperity to the country. Under Nehru's leadership the modernizers won and Gandhian views were given little attention in the official development strategy.

Nehru saw India attaining the levels of economic development achieved by the Western nations through industrialization and modernization. Rational allocation of resources, industrialization, and modernization became the key words in the vocabulary of development during his period. Another strand in his thinking was that the state would play the principal role in initiating development and the market would function under its overall direction The private sector also accepted this formulation and one could say that there was broad national consensus on this issue at that point of time. The consensus was based on agreement among the leaders of the Congress party, influential large industrialists, and technocrats and bureaucrats. Consequently, the discourse on development was formulated in the technical vocabulary of economics, science, and technology. The need of expert advice was strongly felt and the Planning Commission was created in 1950 to provide an institutional forum for its expression.

An effort was made to give the Planning Commission an aura of prestige by establishing it as a technical body consisting of experts who commanded a certain amount of autonomy in decision-making. The power of the Planning Commission flowed from Nehru's own patronage and status granted to it by him becoming its chairman. Nehru entrusted economic development to a small group: over a decade the membership of Planning Commission was drawn from a pool of about 20 men (Khilnani 1997: 81). Most of the members were civil servants but some represented private interests too.

Professional economists and technocrats quickly came to dominate the public discussion about India's economic development. The Planning Commission became the exclusive theatre where economic policy was formulated. The subject was taken away from the cabinet and parliament, which were merely informed of the decisions taken by a small cohort of experts. Khilnani (1997: 86) cites the Second Plan as an instance where political decisions were camouflaged in technical terms to insulate it from public scrutiny. During this period the influence of experts and technocrats rose significantly as they moved in and out of the government effortlessly.

At least three consequences of this strategy need to be highlighted. One was centralization of decision-making. As the decisions regarding development were techno-economic, they were made by the Planning Commission that sometimes even superseded the decisions of the cabinet. The fact that Nehru was chairman of the Planning Commission as well as prime minister allowed the Planning Commission, dominated by economists and technocrats, to concentrate decision-making powers in itself and to send its decisions to the ministries and state governments for implementation. This led to the second consequence, namely the rise in the power of economists and scientists within government and their rise in status in society. A related consequence for the educational sector was the growth of scientific and technical education in the country that provided the manpower for rapid industrialization. While the private sector lagged behind, the increasing pace of investment in public sector industries demanded large numbers of engineers and technicians. The government jobs provided good salaries, security, and status in society.

The rise of the influence of the intellectuals and technocrats in government decision making was facilitated by two factors. The Planning Commission, with its band of experts led by P.R. Mahalanobis, a statistician by training, helped inculcate the belief that science and technology could find solutions to all problems and that the rural population has to be prepared to accept such solutions. Khilnani (1997: 87) points out that science was seen as the key to improved rates of economic growth and as essential for a self-generating economy in industry as in agriculture. This idea coupled with the acceptance of the critical role of the state in triggering development led to a big demand for scientific and technical personnel to handle the public sector and carry such a development strategy forward.

Within government these developments sowed some seeds of conflict. During the colonial rule, generalists had dominated decision-making—a tradition that was imbibed by the successor administrative service. Nehru's intention was to subordinate civil servants to the superior rationality of scientists and economists—the men who came to dominate the Planning Commission. But such favouritism was resented and, in later years when Nehru was no longer on the scene, the Planning Commission became a dumping ground for those civil servants who could not be accommodated elsewhere due to their seniority. In the ministries, all efforts to give greater prominence to technical personnel were limited as the civil servants jealously guarded their key positions.

Nevertheless, for many decades the growth in the supply of scientific and technical personnel was so impressive that the policy planners ignored the disparities being created in the educational system. The goal of universalizing elementary education was so neglected that by 1991 the country had achieved only 52 per cent literacy. Yet, despite the continuing high rates of illiteracy, a large professional group emerged in society. The 1980s and 1990s have seen higher levels of economic development and an expansion in the private sector. In the liberalization phase, multinationals have also entered the Indian market and generated many more jobs for professionals.

As a result, a large middle class consisting of government servants, professionals, and entrepreneurs in the modern sector has emerged. There are various estimates about the size of this class but most agree that it numbers around 200 million. Many scholars and journalists (see particularly Varma 1998) have commented on how this class has acted as a political force in changing public policies to reflect its values and aspirations. One characteristic often mentioned is that the new Indian middle class is Western oriented and holds Western achievements in high regard. Consumption standards for this class are also solidly grounded in globalized Western culture.

More significantly, the middle class agenda places great emphasis on technical solutions for most development problems of the country. Impatient with the humdrum of democracy, insistent demands for rapid action lead to an erosion of optimal decision-making. Led by industrial and business communities, some seek to insulate economic decision-making from day-to-day democracy. It is argued that having periodic elections with a party coming into power on the basis of a manifesto is enough for the functioning of a democratic government. Another manifestation of such impatience is the dropping out from participation from electoral activity. Lower proportions of this class participate in elections or in other political activities.

This new middle class has been very influential in changing public policies during the last decade. In previous decades, poverty and its eradication provided the major part of political rhetoric. This moral concern has now been superseded by an enthusiasm for technology which seems to hold the key to prosperity. Poverty is still on the agenda, but not in the direct way that it had been earlier.

Rusting of the Steel Frame: Bureaucratic Retreat

Indian bureaucracy continues to be heavily influenced by its colonial heritage despite regular criticism that these characteristics are highly inappropriate for the changed circumstances of democracy or for a federal system of government. Likewise, despite acceptance of the view that bureaucratic dispositions and development needs did not match each other so that their mismatch resulted in poor performance, the experience of the post-Independence years indicates that components of the colonial tradition remain well entrenched in the administrative system. Some of these holdover components from the Indian Civil Service (ICS) are:

- Election or, more usually, appointment of professionals to high office;
- Dominance of generalists in policy-making within secretariats at central and provincial levels;
- Extensive controls over policy implementation placed on district officials;
- Separation of policy-making by elite generalists in secretariats from policy implementation by subordinate experts: the old adage 'experts on tap, not on top';
- Frequent rotation of ICS members from secretariat to district positions and back. The purpose of the rotation system was to bring practical experience to policy-making but it also meant much paperwork and noting on files so that each person on arrival at a new post would have the background to the policy issues at his/her fingertips.

Members of the colonial Indian Civil Service had been largely recruited in Britain and consisted of a small band of elite officers who took all decisions of consequence in the administrative system. They were the trusted agents of the British Raj and held all critical positions in the government at field level as well as in the secretariat. Setting aside all strategic posts in government and allowing incumbents only from a small elite service led to strong centralization tendencies in the administrative system. Subordinates had to confine themselves to routine tasks or to preparing detailed case reports so that decisions could be taken by their superior officers.

In the post-Independence period, the ICS was replaced by the IAS which carried on the traditions set by its predecessor. As a matter of fact, the IAS shaped itself in the mirror image of the ICS and over the years the characteristics mentioned above became the distinctive features of the current administration too. But sustaining some ICS traditions was not enough for the IAS to maintain a status and prestige in government similar to that of the ICS. During the past few decades it has lost some of its sheen, particularly after its role during the 1975–7 Emergency period. Many consider this period to be a watershed in the history of the IAS in India.

Until the demise of Nehru, senior civil servants had been seen as partners in development who took major responsibility for implementing planned economic development. Most research conducted during this time was directed at the constrictive role of political leadership and the enabling role of administrators in the planned change being brought about. In the late 1960s, when the initial development programmes were seen to have failed and the Nehruvian model had become suspect, these perceptions began to be reversed. Political leadership indicted administrators for becoming obstacles in development and for not being committed to planned social and economic goals. In turn, the administrators accused the political leadership of interfering in the operation of administration and thus distorting the goals of development. Things came to a pass during the Emergency and, as Das (1998: 146) puts it, 'by the time the Emergency ended, the colonization of the civil service was complete'.

Potter (1996: 156) also noted: 'it was clear to the IAS men whom I interviewed in 1983 both in Delhi and in the States, that in the early 1970s it seemed loyalty to the party in power became part of their reward structure which had not been true before. Those who were loyal were now much more likely to get promotion and desirable postings.' Consequently, when the government changes there is a spate of transfers and it is now accepted that ministers would bring in 'loyal' civil servants to head their ministries. Autonomy and neutrality, well-known characteristics of the ICS, have taken a beating, and the IAS is now seen more in political terms. Due to wide expansion in numbers and policies to encourage recruitment of the deprived groups, the civil service has also lost its social 'elite' character.

While many efforts at structural change have been initiated, little impact has been felt. The near failure of administrative reform needs to be seen in the perspective of the rise in bureaucratic power in which Indian bureaucracy has been relied upon as an instrument of social and economic change in the independent era. The policy planners gave administrators major responsibility for developmental programmes whether in rural areas or the industrial sector. Within the planned economy public sector enterprises were set up in manufacturing, marketing, and the service sectors—all manned by IAS officers. The numbers recruited into the IAS expanded because it now had to staff both the traditional wings of the government as well as the new economic enterprises.

With the IAS holding such crucial positions in the government it was difficult to make a change in its role, particularly when the IAS itself was given the responsibility to bring it about. The 1966–9 Administrative Reforms Commission (ARC) was the last major attempt to adjust administration to its changed circumstances. The ARC made significant recommendations regarding the use of experts, loosening the hold of the IAS officers over critical positions of policy advice in government, setting up policy analysis units in ministries, etc. However, nothing significant on this front ever occurred.

The characteristics of the Indian administrative system do not provide adequate space for technocratic decision-making. The policy-making administrators frequently learn the nuances of the substantive aspects of the job of their ministries through experience after their appointment. In many cases, by the time such learning matures, the official is transferred to another ministry where the learning process has to begin anew. Often transfers take place in the midst of the policy change process itself. When a new incumbent undertakes his/her new responsibilities, the process begins again with repeat briefings from experts who may now have a different view with which to contend. The result is that sometimes the system throws up officers who dedicate themselves to learning with zeal; for most officers it is just another job.

Within such a system, where the administrators are non-experts, extensive consultation becomes the norm for administrative functioning. But because the search is for consensus, an expert opinion—even if it is appropriate—may not be accepted by the administrative group. The civil servants who tend to succeed in India are those who have developed good relational skills, who are adept at sifting technical advice from various sources, and who then have the skills to build a consensus over a view to which they subscribe.

Politicized Cabinets and Non-decision-making

In the parliamentary system of government, the cabinet led by the prime minister is the highest decision-making body in a country. Members of the cabinet comprise the team convened by the prime minister for collective decision-making. They are also ministers in charge of specific ministries or portfolios with responsibility for the effective performance of all departments under them. Ministers thus have a dual role—one as a member of a political collectivity and the other as efficient managers of complex organizations. One would expect a prime minister to seek qualities of both kinds when choosing a cabinet. In addition, it is also assumed that cabinet ministers would provide independent viewpoints but would nevertheless implement whatever is collectively agreed.

The data on cabinet formation in India reveal a varied pattern. The cabinets that have emerged in India have a strong political character but have placed much less emphasis on the administrative capacity of the ministers. The social background of cabinet ministers reveals that few are professionals or specialists. The dominant occupational category is comprised of lawyers plus those who identify their profession as 'social service'. During the pre-Independence days of nationalist struggle, this category played a dominant role. That it continues to be influential is a reflection of the way in which law is chosen as a profession. For most lawyers, law itself is not a choice for legal practice but rather a profession that provides ample opportunity and time to pursue politics.

Ministries are headed by people who are neither necessarily

knowledgeable about the subject-matter nor particularly interested in it. The ministries of education and health, for example, have rarely commanded high status and therefore powerful leaders have not been attracted to them. In many cases, ministers are not interested in these portfolios and care little about what happens in their charge. In the policy field of education, there have been instances when educationists (scholars or former vice-chancellors) were chosen to head the ministry. But in the field of health, only one professional physician has headed the ministry—and that too in the first cabinet after Independence. There are some instances, however, where specialists were incorporated in the cabinet. The Law Department has usually been assigned to lawyers. Another recent example is that of an eminent economist becoming the finance minister. But these are exceptions to the general rule. The common pattern is of ministers with political interests but few professional skills to supervise a department.

Another characteristic of cabinets is that the prime ministers have asserted their leadership in a manner in which independent opinions have not been commonly encouraged. Very early in the history of cabinet functioning in India, conflicts surfaced between cabinet ministers and the prime minister. As Home Minister, Patel once wrote to Nehru deploring the latter's tendency to interfere in ministerial affairs. Patel said that ministers should be free to carry out cabinet decisions and that the prime minister should step in only when disputes arose. Nehru countered that it was his responsibility to maintain the utmost coordination which would not be possible if ministers took important decisions without reference to the prime minister or the cabinet. Patel died soon thereafter and Nehru's interpretation became accepted practice.

This convention was taken to its logical end by Indira Gandhi whose cabinets were reduced to a collection of 'tame subordinates' and the government became a 'one-man show'. A former secretary to the prime minister has described how members of Indira Gandhi's cabinets produced only such proposals as would find favour with her (Alexander 1991). Short tenures and rapid turnover of cabinet ministers have also helped to accentuate this process.

The result is that political factors dominate in the choice of ministers and in cabinet decision-making. The tendency is towards creation of a consensus which takes political factors into account. The civil servants who are advisers to the ministers are generalists moving from one ministry to another. Thus, the distinctive feature of policy-making in India is the predominance of political factors. The leadership gets preoccupied in managing diversities and building consensus in order to uphold national unity and integrity, and concerns for efficiency and technical optimality do not find much space in the decision-making process.

Chapter 4

Health Policy: The Netherlands and India

GOOD HEALTH IS THE cornerstone of hopes for reducing poverty and encouraging economic development. Yet the continuing scarcity of effective health support systems in much of the world permits health problems to proliferate and sharp differences in longevity and mortality rates to persist. Throughout the less developed world, people still suffer unnecessarily due to poor access to medical facilities, shortages of trained personnel, and lack of appropriate, affordable medicines, especially in rural areas. To achieve health for all, it is increasingly clear that the focus of health care should be on the first level of care provided by primary health care centres which stress preventive medicine rather than curative care. Readily accessible basic health care can offer preventive as well as curative help fitted to particular problems of the region—immunization, treatment for diarrhoea, antibiotics, etc. The primary health centre is also the point of entry for referrals to higher levels of health services.

Few problems are more complex or more intractable than finding effective ways to implement development objectives that seek improvement in life expectancy and of the human condition. These problems become even more daunting when the objectives acknowledge the limits of state intervention, yet seek sustainable growth. Pressures of population and resource constraints further compound implementation problems, so that the search for effective methods and efficient systems challenges policy activists and analysts alike. How does the state respond to demands for health and health care? How does it reform and improve the health delivery system for its citizens? Health care provides a classic domain for policies, both public and private, which aim to improve the well-being of people.

The health care sector is defined to include all activities implicit in the 1978 Alma Ata Declaration. These activities may be categorized as follows:

- *Medical care* includes medical relief, which consists of conventional curative medical facilities such as primary health centres and subcentres, hospitals, and dispensaries; indigenous systems of medicine; health insurance schemes for formal sector employees and their families; medical education and research; and direction and administration.
- *Public health* incorporates prevention and control of communicable diseases, health education, immunization, and other public health activities, but excludes water supply and sanitation.
- *Family welfare* includes maternal and child health and family planning.
- *Water supply and sanitation* includes outlays on provision of potable water supplies, sewage, and drainage, and waste disposal facilities in rural and urban areas.
- *Nutrition* covers programmes to supplement nutrition for children plus pregnant and nursing mothers as well as programmes featuring multipurpose children's centers in rural areas.

Under this definition of the health sector, the first item consists largely of spending on curative aspects of the health sector. The remainder can be broadly viewed as preventive health care. Far too frequently, the first item monopolizes attention as if health were identical with medical care services. Like all bad habits, it is difficult to break this simplistic equation. Public policies on health focus almost exclusively on the medical care system (euphemistically called the health care system) rather than on health *per se*, so that public money is spent largely on the delivery of medical services for long-term disabilities as well as short-term treatments. Other than the proverbial hand-wringing rhetoric and futuristic pronouncement, there is very little palpable concern for health in its ecological and holistic dimensions.

The Emergence and Nature of the Dutch Health System

The tension between health policy and health care policy has a long pedigree. Collective arrangements in health care in the Netherlands can be traced back to the Middle Ages when churches, charities, and local governments set up hospitals for the poor, the sick, and the mentally ill (De Swaan 1989). Medieval guilds also initiated financial support schemes for members unable to work and for the widows of their members. These may be seen as an early type of voluntarily organized 'friendly society'. After the Industrial Revolution, eighteenth-century friendly societies and nineteenth-century labour unions and charitable organizations established sickness funds. The interaction between the desire of these funds to aid their low-income members and the increasingly egalitarian philosophy of the government led to extensive debates on the necessity of state regulation during the first few decades of the twentieth century.

In the nineteenth century, selective care for the poor was the only notable social provision from state resources. Article 22 of the 1848 Constitution of the Netherlands stated: 'government shall make arrangements for the benefit of health care'. Children, the unemployed, the disabled, the elderly—all received a contribution in kind small enough to motivate them to join the labour force. Public awareness of health care as a common good and shared interest preceded governmental activity in this sector. On some occasions, private initiatives compelled government to take over certain tasks.

The first explicitly social legislation was passed during the last quarter of the nineteenth century. Focused on the protection of children, pregnant women, and industrial labourers, these laws were weakly enforced (van der Hoeven 1963: 14). In 1904 Abraham Kuyper, a famous Protestant ('anti-revolutionary') politician, proposed the first health insurance legislation, which would have introduced mandatory health insurance for all wage earners under a certain threshold of income. Domestic workers were excluded in order not to upset family arrangements. The proposal covered a wide range of services including medical care, prescription drugs, and income support during illnesses or in case of death. Originally Kuyper wanted an even broader membership for the health insurance, including all low-income groups. When he deemed the latter to be politically infeasible, it was withdrawn. The proposal included the establishment of funds controlled by regional government, and private insurance funds would have been admitted on the condition that they were to be government regulated and would accept all insured persons. This proposal may be seen as the first 'convergence act' in the Netherlands, where the concept of convergence is used to indicate the process in which the difference between sickness funds and private health insurance is gradually disappearing.

The 1904 proposal started a debate about the modalities of social health insurance, which would last for the next ninety years and which has yet to end. All interested parties have joined the debate. Labour unions and employers' associations focused most of their criticisms on the jurisdiction and administration of the funds. Paying the major share of contributions, they felt themselves to be the primary interest groups and claimed exclusive administrative power over the social security funds. They also claimed a majority on the board of the sickness funds. The proposal, however, met firm opposition from the medical profession. In 1908 the Royal Society for the Advancement of Medicine published an 800-page report arguing that physicians should have a much stronger say in the administration of the funds (van der Hoeven 1963: 28). Furthermore, in order to safeguard the freedom of choice for the consumer, the report insisted that all funds should enter into contract with all medical doctors wanting such contracts. In effect, the 'free choice' advocated by the medical professionals meant an unlimited supply of doctors.

Despite this private pressure, it was not until the twentieth century that the Dutch government decided to develop technical capacities and to commit financial resources to support a public health care system (Schnabel 1988: 174). Following Bismarck's example, the liberals began to establish a modern social security system. The 1930 Sickness Law was based on a compromise between employers and labour unions, which provided that industrial associations (*bedrijfs-verenigingen*) rather than the state would manage the implementation of the law. These associations represented the Christian social vision on cooperation between employers and employees as well as subsidiarity or sovereignty in one's own circle. Direct state intervention in health care, however, really began under the German occupation during the Second World War (Björkman and Okma 1997).

Like any health care system, the Dutch system has good and bad points. The former include good-quality care in terms of the level of medical knowledge as well as treatment of patients; equitable distribution of health facilities with relatively easy accessibility to such facilities; and considerable attention to prevention, health promotion, and intersectoral action in the health field. The latter include steadily rising costs; complexities of administering both public and private insurance systems; few incentives for sickness funds to improve efficiency and cost-effectiveness in the health care system; and increasing state regulatory activities. Within this system, organizations of interest groups and welfare institutions are the institutional heritage which provides the arena for the various attempts of the public sector to influence and guide basic policies.

Private initiative still frequently precedes government involvement in the Netherlands. Problem identification is often initiated by private individuals or organizations who subsequently turn to government for recognition and support. Once an issue gets institutionalized, government undertakes its regulation and financial support while private organizations serve as a providers or implementors. External pressures remain important because these strengthen the influence wielded by technical professionals within the administration, whose expertise would otherwise be less relevant in the bureaucratic hierarchy.

The current Dutch health system reflects the history of the power struggle among all these parties. Over time, the system has revealed some remarkable shifts as well as basic continuities. Shifts have occurred from consumer power (the early sickness funds) to medical professionals (as they threatened boycott and blackmail in order to gain influence and 'professional autonomy') and, more recently, to governments (as they felt compelled to regulate markets, thus also protecting interests of medical and other professionals). These shifts in power are also reflected in the institutional theatre of policy-making in the Netherlands.

The health system in the Netherlands is complex, but it can be summarily described as a combination of elaborate government regulation on the one hand and mainly private provision of health care facilities on the other. Consumers, providers, and third party payers (sickness funds as well as private insurers) have organized themselves into federations and peak associations. There are several hundred consumers' and patients' groups which, in turn, are organized into one central federation. Regional authorities have formed a provincial forum, the Interprovincial Platform, as have municipalities in the Association of Dutch Municipalities. Both peak organizations are active in the debates on social security and health care reforms.

As in several other countries of Western Europe, Dutch health care was initially financed by sickness funds, many of which were founded in the nineteenth century. Extensive debates during the first few decades of the twentieth century on the necessity of state regulation led to the expansion of state regulations with the first law on this subject in the Netherlands appearing in 1933. Medical care insurance became compulsory, however, only by decree of the German occupation authorities during the Second World War. Although subsequently codified in law, most features of the imposed system of compulsory health insurance are recognizable today. Insurers, providers of care, and patients bargain within constraints defined by law.

Social and private health insurance provide the largest share of health care financing; about three-fifths of the population are enrolled in one or another of the 25 sickness funds. Sickness fund participation is mandatory for wage earners with incomes below a certain limit, for certain groups of unemployed, and for welfare recipients as well as elderly persons with low incomes. The government sets the contribution rates and the benefits under the sickness fund insurance scheme. In contrast to Germany, contribution rates are uniform for all funds. Some 6 per cent of the population are enrolled by a specific insurance scheme for civil servants, and the remaining one-third may opt for private insurers. Although the latter is voluntary, almost everyone in the Netherlands carries health insurance. Recent estimates show a non-insurance rate of only 1.5 per cent. There are approximately 50 private insurance companies offering health insurance.

A general social insurance covers the expenses of longer term institutionalized and home care. This insurance, the Exceptional Medical Expenses Act (AWBZ), has been part of the Dutch system since 1967. Implemented by the sickness funds and the commercial insurance companies, AWBZ premiums are paid by employers as a percentage of wages. Altogether the social insurance, sickness funds, and private insurance cover some 80 per cent of all expenditures in health care. The remaining 20 per cent are paid out of the government budget and by direct payments by patients.

Administration of sickness fund insurance is decentralized to sickness funds which cooperate in the Netherlands Health Insurance Association. The sickness funds are controlled by a 37-member Sickness Funds Council with representatives from government, providers of medical care, sickness funds themselves, employers and employees, as well as representatives of consumers' and patients' organizations. Being under the supervision of the Ministry of Health, Welfare and Sport, this council is relatively weak because its decisions may be appealed by interested parties and may be suspended or nullified by the government. It reveals one more example of the tightly interlinked, not to say deadlocked, representation of corporatist interests in the Netherlands. In January 1995 the council merged with the peak association of private health insurers into the new organization Health Care Insurers Netherlands.

Many advisory bodies and agencies have specialized in certain aspects of health policies. Some focus on medical technology and ethical issues. Others specialize in advising the government on tariffs and hospital budgets and on the planning of health care facilities and capacities. Their membership also reflects the corporatist tradition because almost all interest groups are represented: labour unions, employers' associations, sickness funds as well as private insurance agencies, organizations of patients and consumers, medical and other professionals in health care, hospitals and other health care facilities, and representatives of the regional and local authorities. In 1992 there were 39 distinct advisory bodies in the health care field (BCVA 1993: 17).

The fragmentation of Dutch society and bureaucracy is reflected in the health care sector. Medical professionals are safeguarded from government control by their specific expertise as well as their traditional autonomy. The distinction between health care as a general interest and as a societal sector has only recently been made. Previously both were perceived to be the same as defined by the members of this sector itself. Government as well as society relied on the expertise of medical professionals and the managers of health organizations.

With depillarization during the 1970s, relationships among providers and consumers of care and particularly the government started to change. Gradually, the dominance of medical professionals and managers shifted to government/allocators and patients/consumers (Schnabel 1988: 174). The independence of health care experts declined. Whereas government once followed professional initiatives in the health care sector, it how began to develop financial and economic policies with important consequences for the medical sector. This change was triggered by the relentlessly rising costs of health care services, particularly in the hospitals and nursing homes. It has to be noted that government did not initiate the direct provision of health care; rather, it started a socio-economic polic of financial constraint aimed at (among others) the health care sector.

The institutional heritage of the Dutch health system is characterized by a plethora of advisory boards, councils, and committees. One of the recommendations of the 1986 Dekker Report had been to reduce the size and number of advisory bodies in the health sector. A shift in decision-making power from the government toward providers of care, insurers, and consumers also implies that there will be less direct government intervention, less regulation, and thus less necessity for advice by external advisory bodies. A follow-up report in 1990, requested by the Deputy Minister of Health, reached similar conclusions (Fortuyn 1990). Both reports advocated a strict separation among the different functions: administration, general policy advice, policy debate between interest groups, supervision, and advice on scientific medical issues. The Sickness Fund Council would limit its functions to the administration of social health insurance, and would include some activities of the Central Organization for Health Tariffs and the Council for Hospital Facilities. The remaining activities of the latter would continue on a privatized basis. There would be an independent body only for supervision, while the National Council of Health would be reduced in size and focus only on the major policy issues.

In late 1993, a letter to Dutch parliament from the Minister of Welfare, Health and Cultural Affairs endorsed the basic arguments for restructuring the advisory agencies. The letter noted that the current structure had excessively interwoven interests that have too much influence on policy making. Furthermore, representation of the different parties is unbalanced because providers are overrepresented while consumers are underrepresented. This intertwining of interests also affects the quality of decision-making by slowing down the decision-making process. Finally, the changing attitudes toward the role of the government involve an expectation of more deregulation as well as a shift in decision-making power from the government toward the other parties. The advising agencies should therefore focus on the major policy issues rather than on detailed matters of actual administration. The letter mentioned three functions: general policy advice; administration of social insurance funds and their supervision; and advice on scientific affairs. The goal of having only one advisory body for each function would involve a reshuffling and curtailing of the existing bodies. This will also restore political primacy over the partial interests of different groups involved in health care.

In 1993 a special Commission of the parliament presented its report, *Raad op Maat* (Measured Advice), on the total range of advisory agencies. It noted the rapid proliferation of advisory bodies with considerable intertwinement of functions, especially in health care, and proposed a drastic reduction of the number of such advisory bodies. The commission mentioned various reasons for such a reduction, including the tight budgetary situation as well as other more fundamental reasons such as a widely perceived need for deregulation and a reduction in the role of government. The commission sought to reduce the direct representation of interest groups and proposed to limit the membership of councils and advisory bodies only to independent experts; it recognized, however, the difficulties in finding truly independent agents. The commission also proposed the end of mandatory advice for all major policy changes. In the future, the government and the parliament may ask for advice rather than having it automatically required or proffered.

Following the commission's report, the government announced a drastic overhaul of the total system of advisory bodies and agencies. As an initial step, the legal requirement for the government to consult the advisory bodies on each and every step in the process of legislation was withdrawn. Next, a drastic reduction in the size and numbers of advisory bodies was announced. As a first step, all existing bodies were to be reviewed and terminated by the so-called 'desert law'. This law also reduced the advisory role of the Sickness Fund Councils but continued their supervisory tasks. Next, new bodies were set up. Originally, it was proposed to set up one committee for each department, but the number was somewhat larger as the new bodies were to cover broad policy areas as their advisory domain. After the 1994 general elections, parliament itself drastically reduced the number of its own specialized committees. In principle, there is only one committee for each government department.

These changes in the structure and functioning of advisory relationships illustrate a further shift in decision-making power from the consumer (at the beginning of this century) toward the medical professionals and health care institutions, and then toward the (central) government. Because budgetary controls necessitate direct government intervention in the planning and control of health care services, the institutional heritage is losing its direct influence. Intermediary and advisory bodies are no longer regarded as platforms for discussions with all interested parties but rather, at least sometimes, as obstructions to quick policy changes.

The increased importance of government in health care does not, however, mean that the policy sector came under government control. Government has been relatively successful in cost containment, but much less in the control of developments in the health care sector itself. Schnabel (1988: 192) distinguishes three powerful groups that he calls the Dutch 'Trias Therapeutica', which parallel the categories described by Alford (1972): corporate rationalizers, professional monopolists, and equal-health advocates. The first group (government and purchasers) steers health care through money and regulations; the second group (medical professionals and managers) manages itself through knowledge and organization, and the third group (patients and outsiders) controls and corrects both the first and the second through information and opinion-making. Schnabel's third category consists of patient-organizations and direct representatives of patients on councils, boards and advisory bodies, but it also includes social (health care) scientists, journalists, medical ethicists, and health care lawyers. All these focus on the health care system without themselves being part of it.

Some observers address the decline of organized power of medical specialists, and suggest that this process has increased technocratic tendencies within the health department. Since the permanent committees have been abolished and because the administrators no longer need to negotiate constantly with the different interest groups (of which medical specialists were by far the most important), there is growing tendency to opt for a quick and mechanical approach—perhaps as an overreaction to the frustrating and time-consuming quests for consensus and compromise of the previous decades. This tendency has yet to be studied extensively so empirical evidence is fragmentary.

As specialized experts, medical professionals and technocrats have always been important in health care. Because of the complexity of its health care system, many advisory organizations and research institutes were created in the Netherlands. When the autonomy of medical professionals began to decline, the nature of expert influence changed. As the government became concerned with cost-containment, the Health Ministry began to recruit economists, legal professionals, and employees with managerial skills. Debate on health-related subjects rarely focused on health care *per se*, but rather on organizational and financial matters. New interest groups such as organizations of patients or specific disease groups added other concerns and expertise, too.

In December 1993, parliament decided to initiate an inquiry into the decision-making process on health care reform. A investigative committee on health decision-making, the so-called Willems Committee, published its report in March 1994. The report contains an analysis of the decision-making process since the publication of the Dekker Report in 1987. It concluded that, from the very beginning, there has been no clear political consensus as a solid base for the restructuring efforts. The various interested parties have shown great reluctance to go beyond their own parochial concerns. The issues have been obscured by hidden agendas and by a lack of precise definitions of the concepts used in the policy debates. Some parties, especially the largest employers' association and the central organization of private insurance companies, have been very vocal and very effective in their opposition.

The arguments of the various interests are reflected in partisan debates as well as in the reports of the permanent and temporary advisory bodies. The Christian Democratic Party has been inclined to support the position of the health care institutions and, in recent years, the employers' association. The Labor Party tends to take up the arguments of labour unions and consumer groups whereas the Liberal Conservatives support the employers' association and the private insurance companies. The Liberal Democrats largely support the government policies.

General elections in the Netherlands held in May 1994 produced a major loss for the two then-governing coalition parties. In September 1994 a new governing coalition consisting of the Labor Party, the Liberal Democrats, and the Liberal Conservatives presented its programme. The new cabinet announced that it would take a different route than its predecessor in the health care reform process. Cost control measures would continue to be based on the existing centralized legislation. These measures include increases in co-payments and deductibles, and limits on the number and scope of services covered by social health insurance. But new laws would focus on the convergence between sickness funds and private health care insurance. The major issues of the coalition's announced programme were:

- Maintaining the existing Exceptional Medical Expenses Act (AWBZ) as a separate funding source for longer term care, rather than integrating it with other health insurance;
- Integrating medical specialists' incomes with the hospital budgets, replacing the existing fee-for-service payments;
- Continuing centralized government planning of health care facilities, and centralized pricing policies;
- Sharpening the anti-cartel legislation in health care;
- Introducing legislation aimed at 'converging' the social and private health insurance systems;
- Increasing cost control measures for drugs; and
- Reducing the coverage of the social health insurance package.

This programme reflects the issues in the earlier debates on health care. It also shows that persistent opposition by different interest groups has greatly influenced policy-making. Groups which would have lost most power or status after full implementation of the Dekker proposals (such as the sickness funds, private insurance companies, AWBZ-institutions, medical professionals, even labour unions and employers' associations) seem to have been especially effective in their lobbying efforts. On the other hand, not all lobbying has been successful. After the 1997 election, the second 'purple coalition' of Social Democrats, Liberal Conservatives, and Liberal Democrats has continued these trends. The system of budgeting the sickness funds has been expanded; the centralized government controls will not allow for greater negotiating power between the insurers and the (AWBZ-financed) institutions; the medical professionals have not regained their automatic right to be contracted by the sickness funds; and measures are underway to further curtail the social insurance package.

Altogether, therefore, the institutional heritage of the Netherlands has provided an operational theater for policy debates and policy making in health care. Characterized by a wide variety of institutions reflecting particular interests and religious groups, the Dutch health care system displays a mixture of elaborate government regulation and private provision of services. Like other European countries, the Netherlands has had a long tradition of collective arrangements in health care services and in health care financing. Government intervention is of relatively recent vintage and limited in its influence by the existing institutions which reflect the power of the major (private) players in the field. The first two decades after the Second World War were characterized by a rapid expansion of health care facilities, followed by two decades of efforts to control expenditures and failed attempts to introduce fundamental reforms.

On an even wider canvas, efforts to introduce comprehensive health care legislation failed for over 90 years due to continuous opposition from various interest groups. The continuing debate reflects an underlying conflict over turf and specifically the question of which party will have authority over the administration of social insurance. The power struggle has been, and is, based on a negative consensus: there is widespread agreement on the necessity of change but, at the same time, there is deadlock in the debate because the various interest groups have created an effective blockage to changes which would affect their positions.

Over time, there have been some shifts in decision-making power. Early in the twentieth century, the original (mutual) sickness funds were based on organized consumers. Then, feeling threatened in their practice and their professional autonomy, the medical professionals organized themselves in reaction to this bargaining power. In the process, they gained influence and effectively blocked the introduction of general health care insurance before the Second World War. During the inter-War period, the government tried to regulate funding and supply, but failed. After the Second World War, power shifted toward the intermediary advisory bodies which incorporate the different interests in health care, with some bias toward the providers. More recently, the Dutch government has tried to gain direct control, by trimming the power of these intermediary bodies, and to increase direct government regulation. The failed reforms of the 1980s imply that there has not been a shift in decision-making power back to the consumer.

To review the historical record, health care ranked low among the priorities of Dutch governments until the end of the Second World War. Since the state largely abstained from health care issues, the field was open to private initiatives. Many private, although often not-for-profit, organizations were established. As the post-War welfare state provided increasing amounts of finance, these organizations made full use of the growth opportunities. The dual results were an unbalanced expansion and an explosion of costs. The Dutch health system was characterized by minimal government interference, a complex financial base, a lack of internal coherence, and a plethora of para- or non-governmental organizations.

The end of this largely *laissez-faire* period came in 1974 when the Dutch parliament rather hesitatingly accepted the ministerial memorandum on the Structure of Health Care, but the end of one period has not necessarily assured the beginning of another. During the 1980s various efforts were made at supply-side management through legislation as well as through advisory bodies. The Dutch government sought to control health costs by reducing the number of hospital beds, requiring generic pharmaceuticals rather than brand-name medicines, restricting the intake of medical students, and so forth. None of these efforts was notably successful. In 1987 the Dekker Committee recommended a thorough restructuring of health system financing, including opportunities for less regulated market activities throughout the health sector. These proposals were widely acknowledged as necessary and the coalition government then in office began to prepare the legislation necessary to implement these reforms. Several laws were passed in parliament. Between 1989 and 1992, AWBZ was expanded to include home care, ambulatory psychiatric care, pharmaceuticals, and medical aids; laws on planning and tariffs were revised; the negotiating power of sickness funds was strengthened by terminating the formerly mandatory contracting of medical professionals by the insurers. However, the restructuring process generated growing opposition and, despite a seemingly realistic timetable of five years for implementation, it was subsequently abandoned (Caljé 1992).

In many ways, decision-making on the Dutch health system lies in a state of limbo. While providing high quality and equitable care, its costs have become politically unacceptable both in financial and regulatory terms. The resolution of these problems in a highly participatory and delicately balanced society is not immediately obvious since no one wants to lose his or her (perceived) advantageous position while everyone has a qualified veto-power to delay, if not prevent, decisions and (even more importantly) implementation of decisions.

Yet, since the beginning of this century, the arena for the health policy debate has displayed continuities as well as discontinuities. Certain elements have remained rather stable, such as the institutional heritage of the numerous peak organizations, professional associations, consumer lobbies, and other interest groups. Other elements have changed. There has been a power shift from the consumers (the original sickness funds) to the providers (dominating advisory bodies), and then from providers to the government (after reductions in the role of the advisory bodies). Likewise, players in the arena are adopting new positions. Mergers have diminished the number of sickness funds while the funds and private insurers are collaborating closely in order to gain strategic market position. Organizations of consumers and patients have gained formal representation and have started to act as informed participants in health care debates. Faced with the changing rules of the game, such as those on contracting, providers display anticipatory behaviour in the organization of their services and are creating strategic alliances with other providers. They are also critically reassessing the efficiency and quality of their services.

The Emergence and Nature of the Indian Health System

Practical experience indicates that policy-makers—whether elected politicians or appointed civil servants—are rarely well-versed in all aspects of a policy or its context. Therefore, they almost invariably appoint committees of experts who, by taking the available research knowledge into account, define and refine the particular problems. One way to comprehend the attempts at health reform in India is to review the many commissions that have been appointed during the past half-century (see Appendix 1 for membership lists). The major committees that discussed health care issues and offered recommendations are, therefore, briefly discussed in serial order. Thereafter, the record of implementing their recommendations is reviewed, with particular attention to both agent and finance.

REFORM PROPOSALS

In 1943, the Imperial Government of India appointed a committee, the Health Survey and Development Committee under the chairmanship of Sir Joseph Bhore, to survey the existing medical and public health facilities and organizations in the country and to make appropriate recommendations for further development. The committee submitted its report in 1946, which recommended the setting up of a unified health authority at the Centre and in the provinces; a unified health authority at the district level; the integration of curative and preventive health services; and the Primary Health Centre as the focal point for providing comprehensive curative and preventive services in rural areas.

This report provided the guidelines for most of the health programmes launched by the governments of India and Pakistan for the first fifteen years after Independence; and it remains remarkably relevant today, over fifty years later. Consonant with the Bhore Committee's recommendations, primary health centres were set up as part of the Community Development Blocks, each with a population of 80,000 to 100,000. The government also launched a number of need-based programmes such as the BCG Immunization Programme (1951), the National Malaria Eradication Programme (1953), and the Dai [a '*dai*' is a traditional birth attendant (or an untrained midwife) at local level] Training Programme as part of the Maternal and Child Health Programme (1956).

Although Western (or allopathic) medical practitioners dominate the Indian health care system, India has several well-established systems of indigenous health care such as *Ayurveda, Unani*, and *Siddha*, which prevailed for many centuries before the arrival of the British. Ayurveda, the better developed of these systems, still has hundreds of thousands of indigenous practitioners. Because the Bhore Committee had neglected to assess the indigenous health systems in any depth, a Committee on Indigenous Systems of Medicine was appointed in 1948 under the chairmanship of Colonel Sir R.N. Chopra in order to consider and recommend necessary steps to improve facilities for research and training in indigenous medicine and thereby to increase their usefulness to the public. The most important recommendation of the Chopra Committee was that both Western and indigenous systems of medicine should be harmonized and synthesized for the purpose of both teaching and medical relief. Uniform curricula were recommended for the whole country such that any weakness in anyone system would be supplemented by strong points of the other systems.

At present there are approximately a half-million *registered* practitioners of traditional systems of Indian medicine. During the 1970s about 7,000 students were admitted annually to the 102 indigenous medical schools comprised of 92 Ayurveda, 10 Unani, and 1 Siddha school (Udupa 1975). In comparison, over 14,000 students were admitted to the 132 allopathic medical colleges in India in 1991 (Ministry of Health and Family Welfare 1992: 53). Both allopathic and ayurvedic doctors are appointed to government primary health centres. However, the allopathic system of medicine is dominant.

In 1959, a second Health Survey and Planning Committee under the chairmanship of Sir Lakshmanaswami Mudaliar was appointed to review all available health facilities in the country and to recommend future health planning. The Mudaliar Committee report in 1961 concluded that, while integration of curative and preventive services was proceeding almost everywhere, medical and public health departments continued to function separately at the district level everywhere except in West Bengal and Rajasthan. Consequently, between 1962 and 1970, a number of national programmes were launched, such as Family Planning, Small Pox Eradication, Leprosy Control, and Cholera Control. For each new programme, workers were trained to deal only with that problem. Thus, separate cadres of malaria workers, vaccinators, sanitary inspectors, and others were trained during the 1960s and 1970s.

In 1972, the first meeting of the Executive Committee of the Central Family Planning Council recommended that steps should be taken for the integration of medical, public health, and family planning services at the peripheral level (Lok Sabha Secretariat 1985: 8). In order to examine and make detailed recommendations on the feasibility of having multi-purpose workers in the field, a Committee on Multi purpose Workers under Health and Family Planning Programme (Kartar Singh Committee) was constituted which submitted its report in 1973. In 1974 the combined National Council for Health and Family Planning accepted in principle the concept of multi-purpose workers for implementation during the Fifth Five Year Plan (1974–9). Twenty-eight districts (out of 400) in six states in India initiated multi-purpose workers' scheme, whereby a single-purpose worker—a leprosy worker, for example—was retrained to handle other diseases as well as to undertake promotional and preventive work in villages.

As a result of a prolonged strike by junior doctors of hospitals in

Delhi during 1974, the Health Minister (Dr Karan Singh) established a committee on Medical Education and Support Manpower. Chaired by the then Director-General of Health Services, Dr J.B. Srivastava, its members included directors of the Indian Council for Medical Research, the Post-Graduate Institute in Chandigarh, the All India Institute of Medical Sciences, the member-secretary of the Indian Council of Social Science Research, and several other Central functionaries. However, as Jeffrey (1988: 187) observed, members from state governments were notably absent. In short, the committee represented the medical elite of India with little linkage to practical health services at district and local levels.

The appearance of the report coincided with the imposition of the 'State of Emergency' by Indira Gandhi, and hence its recommendations about grass-roots initiatives were ill-timed. While the report was accepted in general terms, no moves were made to implement it until the Janata government was elected in 1977. The Janata Party, which came to power in the wake of a voter backlash due to forced sterilizations during the Emergency under Indira Gandhi's Congress party, was reluctant to continue a vigorous family planning programme. The emphasis was changed to voluntary sterilization and the family planning ministry was renamed the ministry of 'family welfare'. The most important step taken during the Janata régime (1977–9) was the introduction of the community health volunteer scheme announced in April 1977, which is described more fully below. India was also a signatory of the 1978 Alma Ata Declaration sponsored by the World Health Organization.

When the Congress party under Indira Gandhi returned to power in 1980, the community health volunteer initiative was accepted as a useful scheme. Indeed, its origins lay in the report of the pre-Janata Srivastava Committee which had convened during the Emergency. In response to the Alma Ata Declaration, the Ministry of Health and Family Welfare issued a report of a working group on 'Health for All by 2000 AD' (25 March 1981). The working group set targets to be achieved by the year 2000: a death rate of 9 per 1,000; infant mortality rate below 60 per 1,000; maternal mortality rate of 2 per 1,000 live births; life expectancy at birth for both sexes of 64 years; only 10 per cent of deliveries with birthweight below 2,500 grams (5.5 lbs); natural growth rate of population of 1.2 per cent per year; family size of 2.3; mean age at first marriage for girls at 18 years; all mothers to receive prenatal care as

TABLE 4.1: AVAILABILITY OF SELECTED HEALTH FACILITIES IN INDIA, 1951–91 (PER 100,000 POPULATION)

Year	*Doctors*	*Nurses*	*Hospital Beds*
1951	17	5	32
1961	21	9	52
1971	27	14	64
1981	29	21	83
1991	47	40	95

SOURCE: Central Statistical Organization, Ministry of Planning and Programme Implementation, New Delhi.

well as trained attendance at delivery; and immunizations for major diseases to cover all the population.

In order to achieve these targets, the existing rural health facilities and personnel had to be substantially increased. Health professionals, social scientists, and rural development activists quickly noted that while the targets *per se* were laudable, the approach was not feasible. A study group was jointly set up by the Indian Council of Social Science Research (ICSSR) and the Indian Council of Medical Research (ICMR) to discuss alternatives to the proposal. 'The Alternative Strategy to Achieve Health for All', proposed in 1981 by the ICSSR/ICMR joint committee, points out that many common illnesses are self-curing and/or self-limiting and need only symptomatic treatment with simple remedies, whether herbal, indigenous medicine, or allopathic. Most illnesses are communicable diseases and can be controlled by preventive measures, readily diagnosed, and treated with cheap and highly effective drugs. The group, therefore, proposed that primary health services be based in the community through training and involvement of community health volunteers (CHV)—one male and one female for each 1,000 population. Supplementary services of guidance, training, and support for preventive and curative activities would be provided by the subcentre which would have two multi-purpose workers and two medical attendants. Each subcentre would have five beds to deal with more common medical and surgical problems including intravenous rehydration, deliveries, minor injuries, and provide facilities for family planning. The group recommended elimination of the category of primary health centres after CHVs and subcentres have begun operating. It argued that the existing primary health centres had a conglomeration of semi-professional and paramedical personnel, who delivered poor medical care and gave no preventive and promotive health care.

In 1982 the Government of India announced a National Health Policy to provide 'Health for All'. This was approved by the Indian parliament at the end of 1983 and has since been the guideline for government action in health care. The policy envisioned the following (Chatterjee 1988: 3–5):

- Major modifications in the existing system of medical education and paramedical training, requiring greater orientation to community health as well as an integrated 'health team' approach;
- Reorganization of the health service infrastructure, requiring decentralization to bring the most needed services closest to the community while encouraging 'individual self-reliance' and 'community participation' along with an 'extension approach' utilizing community health volunteers, paramedical multi-purpose workers, and non-governmental organizations; and
- Integration of health plans with efforts in health-related sectors, as well as with socio-economic development processes such as health education, information systems, essential drug and equipment production, insurance schemes, health legislation, and biomedical research.

The statement also set targets beyond mere 'health facilities established' and 'services delivered' to include such indicators as reductions in mortality, incidence of blindness, increase in antenatal and delivery care, immunization and treatment rates of leprosy and tuberculosis. Fertility control indicators were also included as targets—the birth rate, net reproductive rate, and reduced family size through 'effective couple protection'.

Finally, the National Health Policy was explicit about the essential need for stabilizing the size of India's population. It stated

> Irrespective of the changes, no matter how fundamental, that may be brought about in the over-all approach to health care and the restructuring of the health services, not much headway is likely to be achieved in improving the health status of the people unless success is achieved in securing the small family norm, through voluntary efforts, and moving towards the goal of population stabilisation. (Lok Sabha Secretariat 1985: 36)

Since the 1982 statement of National Health Policy, no major advisory committees on health related policy issues have been appointed at the national level. One major panel (the Hathi Committee) did investigate generic prescription drugs within the broader field of pharmaceuticals, and various state-level committees have examined aspects of the health care system such as the burgeoning of private nursing homes and long-term care clinics. But although the private sector in health has been recognized as a welcome supplement to publicly provided facilities, the professional domain seems to have insulated itself against public intervention. Or perhaps other issues of public policy such as economic liberalization and deregulation consume the finite time available for policy discourse.

INVESTMENT PATTERNS IN HEALTH

It is well known that medical equipment and medicines are often in short supply at government health facilities. In India's successive five year plans and the annual plans, investment in medical services has been declining; hence, the continued lack of adequate medicines, personnel, and physical facilities in a large number of primary health centres all over the country is unsurprising. Inadequate funds make the plan targets unachievable. Governmental expenditure on medical care services has been declining for the past thirty years from 3.3 per cent of the total budget in the First Five Year Plan (1951–6) to 1.8 per cent in the Sixth Five Year Plan (1980–5). The Seventh Five Year Plan (1985–90) spent only 1.7 per cent of its budget on health. During the 1990s there has been renewed emphasis on achieving the targets of 60 per cent couple protection by the year 2000 as well as on constructing a primary health centre for every 30,000 population, but much of the additional expenditure has been targeted for family planning activities.

More positive patterns emerge if the analysis adopts a broader perspective on the components of health. By grouping expenditures on not only medical services but on family welfare, water supply, and sanitation as well, a more favourable picture appears. Total health-related investments in the planned sector have risen from 3.9 per cent in 1951–6 to well over 6 per cent during the Fourth to Seventh Five Year Plans (1969–90). Since then the proportion has declined slightly.

Studies of government health expenditures in India provide both good and bad news. The good news is that from the mid-1970s through the 1980s, governmental spending on health programmes of importance to the poor expanded rapidly. Real per capita government health expenditures nearly doubled in India as a whole. Increases in spending on public health, family welfare, water supply, sanitation, and nutrition were particularly large. The bad news is that these increases came to an end in the early 1990s in the wake of the Indian government's structural adjustment programme. Overall health expenditures continued to rise, albeit slowly, but there was a fall in spending for communicable disease programmes and for health in the poorer states.

Between 1974 and 1990 government spending on health in India expanded rapidly. From 1974–8 to 1986–90 the per capita expenditure on health nearly doubled, rising in real terms from around Rs. 41 to Rs. 75 in constant (1988–9) rupees. Furthermore, the largest increases came in those expenditure categories that are most important for the poor. For example, while expenditures on high technology medical services increased relatively slowly, spending on water supplies and sanitation more than doubled while the amount allocated to nutrition and related child welfare programme quadrupled.

The reasons for the shift in resource allocation were more political than economic or technocratic. The shift was primarily a manifestation of political changes that had begun in the late 1960s. At that time, the senior bosses or 'Syndicate' of the dominant Congress party had installed Indira Gandhi—the seemingly meek daughter of the late legendary Jawaharlal Nehru—as prime minis-

TABLE 4.2: GOVERNMENT PER CAPITA EXPENDITURES ON HEALTH, 1974–90 (IN CONSTANT 1988–9 INDIAN RUPEES)

Category	*1974–8*	*1978–82*	*1982–6*	*1986–90*	*% increase*
Medical services	19.7	24.5	26.7	29.5	150
Public health & family welfare	10.5	12.6	17.4	17.5	167
Water and sanitation	8.9	13.9	19.2	21.0	236
Nutrition	1.4	2.0	5.2	7.1	507
Total	40.5	53.0	68.5	75.1	185

SOURCE: Tulasidhar (1996: 7).

ter in the belief that they could continue to operate as usual behind the scenes. This presumption proved to be a major miscalculation. Indira Gandhi turned out to be an astonishingly adept infighter as well as effective campaigner, and during 1969–71 swept the old political establishment from power in a series of adroit moves (Björkman and Mathur 1996). In the 1971 election campaign, she had found the theme *garibi hatao* (abolish poverty) to be particularly effective for mobilizing support. During the national election of 1971, almost all opposition parties had joined hands for the sole purpose of achieving what they themselves called their one-point programme of '*Indira Hatao*'—that of removing Indira Gandhi from office. Her characteristic reply was: *Kucch log kahate hain, Indira hatao; Main kahati hun, garibi hatao!* (Some people say, get rid of Indira; I say, get rid of poverty!) In a deft turn of phrase, Indira Gandhi had not only almost accidentally coined an election-winning slogan but had made herself a symbol of radical social change. Following the 'Indira Wave' in the 1971 poll results, she removed almost every remaining vestige of independent power within her own political party.

In adopting this slogan as her rallying cry, she raised expectations that would have to be fulfilled if she were to be a viable candidate in future elections. Therefore, once settled in office, Indira Gandhi set about initiating a series of anti-poverty programmes, including health programmes. The decisiveness of her electoral victory allowed her to do so with unusual effectiveness because of the unprecedented influence she was able to exercise over state governments (which constitutionally control most public expenditures on health) as well as on the Central government. This situational power allowed her to be much more effective than any of her predecessors in changing resource allocation patterns, not only to benefit the poor but also to enhance her re-election prospects.

Rather than by taking funds from some programmes and giving to others while keeping the total funds constant, the government achieved the shifts in allocations by sharply increasing the overall amount of funds available for health. The strategy adopted featured the establishment of highly visible and politically popular new programmes covering primary health care, water and sanitation, nutrition, and the like in addition to those that already existed. By increasing the total volume of health resources by the amount necessary to ensure that none of the existing programmes suffered, the authorities met the financial needs of these new programmes. The major existing programmes also benefited. Even the least favoured major health expenditure category—medical care services—received some 50 per cent more funds in real per capita terms in the late 1980s than in the mid-1970s. In other words, Indira Gandhi too opted for the path toward reallocation traditionally favoured by political leaders eager to avoid making unnecessary enemies: she spent more.

Spending more may be the easiest way to reallocate, but it can continue for only so long. By the early 1990s the Government of India found itself in serious financial trouble: the budget deficit amounted to more than 8 per cent of the gross domestic product, inflation was up, and foreign reserves were down. Something had to give. By this time, of course, neither Indira Gandhi nor her son and successor Rajiv Gandhi were on the political scene; both had been assassinated in 1984 and 1991, respectively.

One of the many things that 'gave way' was Central government expenditure on health. However, the cuts were not as dramatic as the sharp rises during the preceding fifteen years. Furthermore, the Central government reductions were not matched by cuts in funds allocated to health by state governments, whose resources represent some 80 per cent of total government health spending. Thus, overall spending at the state level continued to increase, if only marginally. Moreover, the Central government cuts may prove to have been only temporary. Recent information points to a restoration of health funding back toward its 1990–1 level.

The impact, however, has been noticeable. The shift in trend stands as clear evidence of a change in Central government priorities. It also had a noteworthy direct impact on funding for programmes in India's poorest areas and for communicable diseases, which are of particular importance for the poor. Central government funds were concentrated in these areas, particularly through its patterns of subsidies or grants to the state governments. Such Central government grants were particularly important for the poor states, whose overall health expenditures fell by 5 to 10 per cent during the early 1990s, while spending in the middle- and upper-income states continued to grow. In the states as a whole, public spending on curative medical services continued to increase, while the allocation to communicable disease prevention and control activities declined by nearly 15 per cent (Tulasidhar 1996:

TABLE 4.3: PER CAPITA PUBLIC EXPENDITURES ON HEALTH, 1974–90 (IN CONSTANT 1988–9 INDIAN RUPEES)

Category	*1974–8*	*1978–82*	*1982–6*	*1986–90*
1. State government expenditures from own resources	30.67	38.38	48.99	55.60
2. State government expenditures from Central government grants	5.76	8.49	13.66	13.31
3. Aggregate state government expenditures (1 + 2)	36.43	46.87	62.65	68.91
4. Central government direct expenditures	4.10	5.06	5.81	6.15
5. Aggregate public expenditures (3 + 4)	40.53	52.93	68.46	75.06

SOURCE: Tulasidhar (1996: 5).

10–11). Thus the modest overall shift in funding affected the poor with unusual severity.

The significance of these findings for India's poor illustrates the value of studying government health expenditure patterns and trends with care. Knowledge about these patterns and trends provides an important complement to official policy statements and ministerial proclamations in assessing governmental priorities. Expenditure patterns and trends do not tell the whole story of priorities, of course, but for those who believe that actions speak louder than words, an understanding of expenditures is even more important than knowledge about policy statements in determining a government's true position.

In India, words and deeds have generally moved *in tandem*. In the 1970s and 1980s, Indira Gandhi's government announced loudly and clearly that it meant to help the poor. Then, in a move that no doubt surprised those who dismiss government pronouncements as political rhetoric, it did what it had said it would do. Later, in the early 1990s, the government began preaching the need for austerity, and this austerity showed up in its expenditure pattern. Such close correspondence between expenditure and stated policy is far from inevitable. In many settings, it is difficult to resist the impression that governments' political statements are far removed from reality. The only way to understand fully what is happening is to study governmental health expenditures carefully.

Given these financial trends as well as shifts in government pri-

TABLE 4.4: PATTERNS OF GOVERNMENT EXPENDITURE ON HEALTH IN INDIA 1985–6 TO 1995–6 (PERCENTAGE)

Year	*Plan expenditure*	*Non-plan expenditure*	*Total govt. expense*
1985–6	2.33	5.54	7.87
1990–1	1.77	4.62	6.32
1995–6	1.83	4.02	5.85
1998–9	1.71	3.81	5.52

SOURCE: Indian Fiscal and Social Monitor, *Indian Fiscal Journal*, vol. VIII, nos. 10–12, 1998.

orities, reforms in the immediate future are likely to focus on the public–private mix in health care. India's private health care sector is both more important and less effective than generally recognized (Bhatt 1993: 43–56). As in many other countries, policy makers in India are becoming increasingly aware of the fact that private health care sector merits greater attention than it has thus far received. India's private health care sector includes a wide range of service providers, some of whom offer modern or Western (allopathic) medicine, others specialize in one or more of several traditional Indian systems of medicine; some operate commercially or for a profit, others are non-governmental or non-profit service organizations. Usually the term 'private service providers' signifies those offering Western medical care for a profit; it excludes not-for-profit arrangements, whether voluntary or non-governmental.

Many factors contribute to this growing awareness. Rising incomes result in the rapid emergence of a middle class, the members of which use some of their increased incomes to purchase health services from private providers rather than go to government clinics. The rise of the middle class thus leads to a comparable rise in the private health care sector. Also, attitudes have changed about the appropriate role for government in providing social services. Part of this change is rooted in contemporary thinking about economic policy, where the advocates of private enterprise have been gaining steadily over those favouring government direction. These ideas have begun to infiltrate the health sector and to permit a more sympathetic attitude toward private services. Finally, there has been a growing recognition among health officials that they cannot 'do it all alone' and that their traditional objective of providing free services to the entire population is beyond their grasp. They are thus open to alternatives, and the involvement of the private sector is one obvious possibility.

Effective involvement of the private sector is not easy, however, and poses new challenges for government policy-makers. It means that ministry officials, in addition to being expected to manage their own programmes effectively, are being called upon to guide and encourage the delivery of services by others. For most, this role is new and unfamiliar. Many realize that they need to understand the private health care sector much better if they are to play this role well.

India's situation is instructive because its private health care sector, while generally believed to be quite large, has until recently been generally marginalized by government agencies more intent on extending their own services. According to some sources, there are nearly three times as many physicians in private practice in India as in government service. The number of hospitals in the private commercial sector is also greater than the number owned and operated by governmental agencies (Björkman 2001).

The private health sector is equally large when measured in financial terms. Indian households spend more than Rs. 50 billion (US$ 1.7 billion) annually for health care. Almost all of this out-of-pocket payment goes to the private sector which is broadly defined to include practitioners of traditional Indian systems of medicine as well as the modern (Western/allopathic) medical sector. This amount, estimated to be three-quarters of India's total health expenditures (Berman 1998: 1465), is much more than the governmental health expenditure and represents a significant burden for consumers, particularly poor consumers, because less than 10 per cent of it (expenditure) is covered by insurance.

Perhaps predictably, private health care facilities are concentrated in urban rather than rural areas. Oddly enough, the urban bias is in some respects less marked for the private health care sector than for the government health care sector. In 1987, for example, some 70 per cent of private hospital beds were in urban areas and 30 per cent were in rural areas. The comparable figures for government hospital beds were 90 per cent and 10 per cent. Likewise, the private health care sector is much more prominent in some regions of India than in others. The determinant appears to be economic development, for advanced states have larger percentages in private practice whereas in remote states and backward territories most physicians are in government service while the private practice of medicine is limited or virtually non-existent. The patterns holds for the relative distribution of public and private hospital beds.

The study of investment in health in India is a comparatively new area. Recent studies (Duggal et al. 1992; Panikar 1992; Berman and Khan 1993) indicate that although socialized medicine is still seen as the basic approach to 'health care for all', the norm is private health care based on high fees. These studies show that India, for its level of income, has a relatively high level of spending on health care, both public and private. A World Bank Report *India: Health Sector Financing* set out to offer an alternative policy framework to cushion the impact of structural adjustment programmes on health services. This has been criticized as suggesting more centralization of health services to make them more equitable and efficient while the country itself is moving towards more decentralized administration (Banerji 1993).

Another area in health care financing that lags behind is health insurance. The lack of a health insurance system in a country as poor as India defies comprehension. Experts feel that though health insurance would be the best option from the consumer's point of view, the highly regulated nature of the insurance industry has hampered the development of successful health insurance schemes. At present only about 5 per cent of India's population is covered by any type of health insurance schemes, leaving a huge potential market for foreign insurance companies to covetously eye. India's first preventive health insurance scheme—Good Health and Cancer Control—has been launched by the Cancer Patients' Aid Association in association with the New India Assurance Company. Not only does this scheme play a role in the control of cancer, but it scores well over other conventional health insurance policies because it provides a free update on the total health status every year (Subramaniam 1995).

HEALTH CARE FACILITIES AND PERSONNEL: MEASURES TO IMPLEMENT HEALTH POLICIES

Programme implementation requires adequate planning and training of change agents, including financial outlays to meet the targets. The success of any health programme depends on the kind of change agents that are recruited and trained (Björkman and Schulz

1981). Often the government formulates programmes which the existing personnel are expected to implement. Since government employees cannot be hired and fired, they are usually reassigned and retrained to handle the new schemes. Much more rarely, totally new schemes have entailed the recruitment of totally new change agents to implement them.

Even though India trains over 12,000 medical doctors per year, almost one-fifth (4,454 or 17 per cent) of the total of 26,723 sanctioned positions of doctors in rural areas were lying vacant in December 1983 (Rajagopalan 1984), while 18,499 medical graduates were on the live register of unemployment exchanges as of December 1982 (*Hindustan Times*, 15 March 1984). The number of unemployed medical personnel is constantly rising. According to the Government of India's Bureau of Health Intelligence (1993: 90), in 1988 there were 30,447 medical graduates, 34,207 pharmacists, and 13,520 nurses on the live register of unemployment exchanges. Medical graduates generally resist employment in rural areas due to poor salaries, inadequate facilities for children's education, and the opportunity to earn more money by practising medicine in urban areas or by migrating to other countries.

Due to the lack of funds and administrative inefficiency, government hospitals themselves are often dangerous to health (Chowdhury 1983). In any case, because of the high correlation between poverty and morbidity (Djurfelt and Lindberg 1975), major reductions in morbidity cannot be expected merely by setting up more hospitals or by training more doctors and paramedical personnel. Many health problems are related to malnutrition, unsanitary environment, ignorance about health practices, nutrition, childcare, etc. Remedies for these lie not in providing more drugs or doctors but in improving the economic, environmental, and educational standards of people. Along with these, aspects of life directly related to health must also be improved.

Population Control: National Family Planning Programmes

Controlling population growth has long been recognized as a major task in the development of India. The growth rate of 2.2 per cent per year during 1970–80, which declined to 2.0 per cent during 1980–93 and which is projected to become 1.8 per cent in the period 1993–2000, is still high for a developing country such as India. Based on current population growth rates, India will overtake China in population size during the twenty-first century.* Some of the obstacles in achieving a lower rate of population growth are early marriage, preference for male offspring by most Indians, and the advantages of having a large family in a non-mechanized agrarian economy.

India is the first developing country to have launched an official population control programme. The dangers of uncontrolled population growth were known to the planners of independent India. A modest beginning was made during the Second Five Year Plan (1956–60) with an average of about 14,000 vasectomies and 16,000 tubectomies per year. Because these rates were far too low to make any impact, the National Family Planning Programme was launched in 1962. In the Third Five Year Plan (1961–5), an average of over 213,700 vasectomies and 60,900 tubectomies were performed annually. These figures rose to 1.27 million vasectomies and 115,000 tubectomies during the inter-Plan period (1966–8). Various approaches were used to encourage and promote birth control measures. Similar to the traditional *mélas* (festivals) to honour deities, family planning *mélas* have been organized in some parts of the country and have proved to be popular. Incentives are given to those who undergo sterilization as compensation for lost wages. During the past forty years, there has been enormous change in plan allocations for the family planning programme. While a mere Rs. 10 million was spent on family planning during the First Five Year Plan (1951–6), a staggering Rs. 68 billion was spent during the Seventh Five Year Plan (1985–90) which amounted to 1.75 per cent of total plan allocation. However, the outlay for family welfare programmes during the Annual Plan of 1991–2 declined to only 1.0 per cent of total plan outlay.

A new thrust to birth control programmes appeared during the 1975–7 period which is now known as the 'Emergency' when Prime Minister Indira Gandhi adopted strong measures to implement government schemes. Her younger son, Sanjay Gandhi, although not a member of her cabinet, was reputedly the force behind the

*By 2050, with an expected 1.533 billion people, India will exceed China's projected total of 1.517 billion. By the end of the next century, the Indian population may have grown to 2 billion, more than double the present 950 million. *The Economist* (22 February 1997: 71).

compulsory sterilization drive launched throughout India during this period. Targets were fixed for every type of government employee including school teachers, revenue officials, and medical staff. During this period, there was a significant increase in the number of sterilizations, with numbers reaching 2.1 million vasectomies and 1.2 million tubectomies per year.

Although unreported due to press (self)censorship, there was considerable resentment about the undue force exerted in many cases to achieve targets of sterilizations, especially in the northern states known as the 'Hindi belt'. The stunning electoral defeat of Indira Gandhi and her Congress(I) party in the March 1977 elections is largely attributed to these excesses. The Janata Party which came to power in 1977 advocated a completely voluntary approach in the adoption of birth control measures. There was an 81 per cent drop in the number of vasectomies and 9 per cent drop in the number of tubectomies the very next year. After 1977 sterilization came to be increasinly used only by women (Caldwell et al. 1984; Srikantan et al. 1984). However, official data are now presented without disaggregation between vasectomies and tubectomies so that it is difficult to assess the extent of 'feminization' of sterilization as a birth control measure.

MATERNAL AND CHILD HEALTH (MCH)

Infant mortality rates in India remain comparatively high. Many infant deaths are related to unsanitary practices at delivery by the traditional birth attendant. Some of the complications such as low birthweight are due to malnutrition and inadequate care of pregnant women. Children between three months to five years old are victims of diseases such as diphtheria, whooping cough, tetanus, and polio. All these are preventable with immunizations. Likewise, pregnant women often have vitamin-deficiencies because local custom deprives them of many nutritious food items.

Based on recommendations of the 1981 committees on 'Health for All' and 'Alternative Strategies', India's 1982 National Health Policy decided that MCH problems can be most efficaciously addressed by training *dais* in sanitary birth practices, nutrition education for pregnant women, and immunization of new-borns and children. Having been initiated in 1956 with reference to the famous Bhore Committee, this programme was less 'reform' than reorientation. Nonetheless, the advantages as well as the liabilities of these indigenous 'providers of health care' merit brief review.

The *dai* is a well-known figure in Indian life. She plays an important role in the life of women, particularly in rural areas. Even today, with the extension of medical facilities to rural areas, only about a half of all deliveries occur in hospitals or are attended by trained nurses or nurse-midwives; the indigenous village *dai* continues to provide obstetric care. The *dai* not only assists at the time of birth, but also counsels village women during pregnancy and after delivery, in times of illness, and when they have personal or domestic problems. She is thus a welcome visitor in the house and wields considerable influence over rural women. Indigenous *dais* have pursued their profession by using traditional and orthodox methods which have been handed down from mother to daughter. Most *dais* are illiterate, and the lack of proper skills and the absence of aseptic techniques in their work lead to high morbidity and mortality among mothers and new-borns.

It was, therefore, felt that this vast potential of indigenous *dais* could be better utilized for extending maternal and child health services to the rural areas by providing them with the necessary training. Such training would not only improve conditions for safe childbirth but also ensure the extension of better maternal and child care services. In addition, the services of the *dai* could be utilized for spreading the message of the small family norm. This was the rationale behind the Dai Training Scheme which was introduced during the Second Five Year Plan (1956–61) period as a centrally sponsored scheme under the Maternal and Child Health Programme. The scheme was continued in successive Five Year Plans up to 1977 in a modest way, but then was re-emphasized during the Janata Party's programme for Community Health Workers (see below)—especially for recruiting female volunteers.

From the inception of the family planning programme, trained *dais* were asked to recruit adopters of family planning. Each *dai* was paid a small cash incentive for each adopter recruited. Since the *dai* was used for massage even by elite women (some of whom would already have regularly had their deliveries in hospitals), she was expected to be a major recruiter of IUD adopters. However, their effectiveness as family planning recruiters was disappointing. The average *dai* persuaded only one IUD acceptor per month. Rogers and Solomon (1975: 26) list a number of reasons for the failure of *dais* to be effective change agents. First, *dais* were of very low social status, often belonging to the barber and sweeper castes. Hence, they were considered polluting by the majority of the rural women. The few women they managed to persuade usually belonged to their own castes. It was almost unheard of for *dais* to talk to men about family planning. Second, the *dais* were given a very brief training course, with the main emphasis on improved methods of child delivery; this was inadequate to prepare them for family planning duties. Thus, in the eyes of their clients, they had neither recognized competence nor complete credibility. In some instances, the *dai's* instrument kit made her stand apart from her clients, undermining her reputation for safety measures as well (Abraham 1977). And third, the immediate supervisors of the *dais* were often government auxiliary-nurse-midwives (ANMs) in local clinics, who were usually young unmarried women with some high school education and two years of training in public health and family planning. The *dais* seldom had much respect for their young supervisors. Also, the incentive payments may have been too small to offset the loss of the *dai's* child delivery fees. In some cases, the *dais* even spread anti-IUD rumours, leading to doubts about the credibility about the safety of proposed methods as well.

Despite all these drawbacks, trained *dais* have been found to be relatively successful as promoters of primary health care at village level. The 'Alternative Model of Health Care' proposed by the ICSSR/ICMR joint committee had recommended the proper training and utilization of *dais* in rural medical care (ICSSR/ICMR 1981: 107). The Dai Training Scheme was vastly expanded from April 1977 along with the Community Health Volunteer Scheme, with the ultimate target of one trained *dai* in each of the 580,000 villages in the country by 1983 (Ministry of Health and Family Welfare 1980). According to the Ministry of Health and Family Welfare (1990: 231), a total of 585,000 *dais* were trained between 1974 and 1990. In the absence of trained medical help during delivery, the presence of *dais* may be better than having no help. Nonetheless, their effectiveness as an important change agent in rural health care may be overstated.

The Community Health Worker Scheme: 'Health Guides'

The Community Health Worker Scheme is the most important scheme as far as rural health and people's participation are concerned. It was announced by Raj Narain—the controversial health minister in the newly elected Janata government—on 20 April 1977 soon after he took charge. Narain announced the Community Health Worker Scheme whereby one male or female worker per village or per 1,000 people would be trained to administer medicines for minor ailments as well as carry out promotional and preventive health care within the village. Said to be India's version of the 'barefoot doctor' in China, some hailed this radical scheme while others questioned the feasibility of training such a large number of people in so short a time.

In its 1977 annual conference the Indian Medical Association (IMA), the organization of allopathic physicians in India, openly registered its opposition to the scheme. A spate of editorials and articles in newspapers and magazines appeared which suggested that the government was 'abandoning the health of the rural poor to quacks'. Deliberations at the IMA conference suggested that medical doctors were the only persons competent to take care of the health of the people; if doctors were unwilling to serve in rural areas under existing conditions, larger financial incentives should be provided.

The medical fraternity was not alone in expressing negative views. Even those agencies chosen to implement this experiment were somewhat skeptical. In the words of one district health officer:

> The scheme (for community health workers) is a premature baby. Its survival requires a lot of special care, but who can give that kind of care? We in the health department barely have enough time to supervise our own staff . . . the idea is good, no doubt, but a seed is only as good as the soil into which it is put. Someone should be there for the weeding. (Nichter 1980: 37)

Such pessimism on the part of the authorities who were to implement the scheme may have been warranted due to the haste with which the scheme was announced and due to the 'crash programme' through which it was implemented.

But the fact remains that Karan Singh, the health minister in the Congress ministry before the Janata government came to power in

1977, had shown interest in the successful experiments by a number of voluntary organizations in the effective training and utilization of village health workers. Thus, Raj Narain only accelerated something already being planned by the health ministry for possible implementation. Of course, had it not been for the sudden announcement and associated political prodding, it may have taken much longer for the bureaucracy to come up with something to implement.

As often occurs with hurried efforts, the Community Health Worker Scheme did not really succeed as planned. The Janata government itself was in power only for thirty months. A number of evaluation studies noted that the scheme, though well-intentioned and with great potential, had serious problems (Maru 1983). Women comprised less than 10 per cent of the community health volunteers selected and trained, which made it difficult to reach the main target groups in rural health care—women and children. Less attention was being paid to prevention, promotion, maternal and child health, nutrition and health education, with greater attention going to family planning. Thus, the main impact of community health volunteers was in the area of family planning persuasion.

When Indira Gandhi returned to power in 1980, this 'trademark' programme of the Janata Party could have been terminated. Instead, it was renamed and integrated into the 1982 National Health Policy. The *Annual Report of the Ministry of Health and Family Welfare, 1981-82* (1982: 19) quietly noted:

> During 1981, as a result of evaluation and concurrent reviews, the Community Health Volunteer Scheme has been completely restructured and revised and [is] now known as the 'Health Guides Scheme'. In the revised scheme, greater emphasis has been laid on the involvement of the community. Provision has been made for the establishment of a Village Health Committee for each village. It is envisaged that this Committee would take an active part in implementation of Health and Family Welfare and MCH programs. Emphasis has been laid on selecting women as Health Guides.

Most states have preferred the scheme of having one male and one female health worker per village. Uttar Pradesh alone appointed only women as health workers. By 1989, almost all the primary health centres of the country were covered under this scheme and 4,10,000 health guides had been trained (Ministry of Health and Family Welfare 1991: 200). The introduction of these volunteers in villages may well have contributed to the decline in infant mortality rates in India from 127 per 1,000 live births in 1978 to 80 in 1993. In some states like Kerala the infant mortality rate has declined to 16. Furthermore, the emphasis of the government on appointing more women as health guides is an encouraging sign as it is now widely accepted that greater involvement by women is associated with significant improvements in the health status of a village community.

Primary Health Centre

One of the major suggestions of the Bhore Committee was to use a primary care approach to address health problems of the vast rural population. That was the beginning of primary health centres where the minimum facilities to take care of the most common health problems would be available. The first primary health centres were set up in 1952 and they remain the mainstay of the rural health care delivery system of the government. Most recently, the goal of providing 'Health for All by 2000 AD' aimed at providing one primary health centre for every 30,000 people (Ministry of Health and Family Welfare 1981). More and more functions have been added to the primary health centre from its inception (van der Geest et al. 1990).

In 1962, the National Family Planning Programme was launched with a doctor specially allocated for that purpose at the primary health centre, making it simultaneously the family welfare centre as well. The Community Health Volunteer Scheme, which was initiated in 1977 with an emphasis on maternal and child health, was put under the charge of another doctor, thus increasing to three the number of doctors at a primary health centre. In the 1960s a number of disease eradication programmes were launched with workers being trained to handle the tasks of detection, distribution of medicines, follow-up, etc. Thus, there were malaria workers, leprosy workers, and sanitary inspectors, all with their own tasks. In the 1970s it was felt that some of these workers were overworked while others were underutilized, so it was decided to train the single-purpose workers into multi-purpose workers capable of handling all aspects of primary health care. Besides the three doctors, paramedical staff such as nurses, ANMs, multi-purpose workers, and sanitary inspectors are attached to the primary health centre.

As a brief summary of the agents through which health policies are implemented in India, health care is provided primarily by three sectors: government, private, and voluntary. First, the government sector has hospitals in cities and district headquarters along with some 22,441 primary health centres and over 1,31,318 subcentres in rural areas (Central Bureau of Health Intelligence 1992: 103).

Second, the private sector operates hospitals and nursing homes as commercial enterprises aimed at profit, mostly in large and small cities. In addition to licensed practitioners from different systems of medicine, it also includes an enormous but unenumerated number of unregistered and often unqualified providers of ambulatory care throughout the country (Berman 1998; Kakar 1988). Non-allopathic (non-Western) systems of medicine—Ayurveda, Unani, Tibbi—operate in an autonomous political realm because, after initial efforts to integrate them into the dominant system, it had been politically agreed to divide public resources among them (Brass 1972).

Third, there is a voluntary sector run by non-profit trusts and associations mostly under the auspices of Christian churches as well as those run by other religious communities. Nearly two-thirds of the hospitals are run by private or voluntary organizations even though they provide only one-third of the total number of hospital beds. It is also interesting to note the absence of hospitals run by private and voluntary agencies in large states such as Madhya Pradesh and Rajasthan, both of which have low health status on almost all indicators. By contrast, the high health status of Kerala may well be linked to the availability of health care facilities, especially in the private and voluntary sector (Panikar and Soman 1984). The relationship among these three sectors is being defined on an *ad hoc* basis.

The institutional set-up for health care in India reflects the recommendations of the Bhore Committee Report of 1946. Little change has occurred on the reliance on primary health centres to provide basic health services at the village with the district hospitals providing specialized support. Other programmes that have been introduced have been additional tasks of the health bureaucracy so created. A large number of vertical programmes like malaria eradication, TB and leprosy control, etc., have also been introduced with Government of India funding, which has brought in its own bureaucracy. This has been in addition to the health policy thrust of family planning (now renamed family welfare) which has gradually burgeoned into a large establishment.

Little integrative assessment of these developments qua policy have taken place after 1982 when the National Policy of Health for All was announced. A respondent characterized 'the health policy as a warfare model where battles are fought but strategies for winning the war are rarely taken up'. In 1998 the Voluntary Health Association of India (VHAI) presented a voluminous report of an Independent Commission on Health in India to the Central government. This was a voluntary effort to have a comprehensive look at health policy after the government had issued its 1982 policy statement. The report contained more than 350 recommendations based on the experiences of a number of non-governmental organizations working in the field and was shaped after extensive discussion. To say the least, the government response was not encouraging. In a letter to VHAI, the Joint Secretary in the Ministry of Health referred to the tremendous effort that the government was already making by initiating new programmes and then went on to defend government policy. The letter sought to absolve the government of its failures by suggesting that 'a responsive and conscious user will be able to revitalize the sector and make it more accountable than what structural changes might be able to achieve' (Government of India letter to VHAI, 18 January 1993: 3).

Chapter 5

Education Policy: The Netherlands and India

THE EMERGENCE AND NATURE OF THE DUTCH EDUCATION SYSTEM

EDUCATION IN THE Netherlands has a long history. The first piece of educational legislation—the Elementary Educational Act—was passed in 1801 and laid the foundations for a national education system. During the nineteenth and early twentieth centuries, education became compulsory and increasingly secular. Elementary schools were divided into public schools funded by the government and private schools funded by private sources. This financial distinction led to the 'schools dispute', which was a political battle to achieve equality for both types of schools. Catholics and Protestants wanted their own schools to retain a pronounced Roman Catholic or Protestant identity but with equal state funding. The Liberals supported equal financial treatment for public and private schools. A pact known as the 'Pacification of 1917' settled the school dispute. Since then, religious *versus* public education has not been perceived as a church–state issue and continued governmental support of church-related schools has never been challenged (Blanken 1976: 148). Subsequently, financial support was extended to secondary and higher education, and there are now almost twice as many privately run schools as publicly run ones.

The 1917 pact agreed that groups in society would have the right to found schools on the basis of their own religious, ideological, or educational beliefs. Article 23 of the Dutch Constitution guarantees the freedom to found schools, to organize their curricula, and to determine the principles on which they are based. The Constitution places public and private schools on an equal financial footing. Consequently, government expenditure on public education must be matched by spending on private education. The conditions that private schools must satisfy in order to qualify for funding are laid down by law. All schools, public as well as religious, receive funding based on pupil ratios.

The Ministry of Education, Culture and Science frames qualitative standards, requirements, and curricula that are equally mandatory upon all schools. These standards, which apply to both public and private education, prescribe the subjects to be studied, the attainment targets, the examination syllabi and content of national examinations, the number of teaching periods per year, the required teacher qualifications, the influence of parents and pupils in school matters, planning and reporting obligations, and so on. The inspection of education is carried out under the minister's authority by the Education Inspectorate, a decentralized service outside the ministry.

Education in the Netherlands has always been organized nationally (by the ministry) rather than at the municipal level. However, there is an increasing trend at all levels of education towards fewer rules and regulations from the national government (Schuler et al. 1996: 1). This is evident in the freedom permitted to schools and institutions in designing programmes of study, for which in many cases only broad guidelines are given. Laws on education provide the necessary framework in varying detail to regulate matters ranging from the educational objectives of a particular programme, through admissions requirements, to funding levels. Deregulation has recently been accompanied by decentralization of responsibilities from the national to the municipal level.

One's perception of whether the trend in the Netherlands has been toward fewer or more regulations is, of course, partly due to partisan perspective. A prominent parliamentarian of the Conservative Liberals (VVD) party argued that the volume of regulations has been growing and cited the story of a young bureaucrat who had a 'quota' for the number of regulations to issue in a specific field during the year. While this is only anecdotal evidence, even without quotas or targets, the annual accretion of rules and regulations slowly builds up to a formidable mass. And there has been no evident effort to weed out regulations in health or education nor to review and consolidate them. In broad terms, however, school standards in the Netherlands are restricted at the national level to the Dutch language and to mathematics, but for nothing else! Through decentralization, discretion for content of all other subjects remains with the local schools.

Government regulations notwithstanding, schools have managed to remain relatively autonomous. As in the health sector, the subsidiarity principle functions as the guiding principle for the organization of duties and responsibilities in the education sector. While regulatory and budgetary powers give the national government much control, local public and private schools have considerable autonomy. Safeguards were written into the education legislation in order to protect the traditional patterns of freedom of religious and private schools.

The Mammoth Law of 1967, a law on secondary schooling, stimulated autonomy even further. It aimed at the establishment of innovations for educational improvement by the local school boards that were operating under considerable freedom. It was anticipated that parent/teacher associations as well as interest and religious groups in non-public schools would be responsible for the annual reports to the ministry. Teacher groups cooperated with government representatives to form 'pedagogical centres' in order to research, improve, and implement educational advances. Organized along the now familiar *verzuiling* or pillar pattern, they participated with others in the government's National Planning Procedure Committee through such organizations such as the Catholic School Committee, Union of Protestant Schools, Foundation for the Promotion of Public Education, General Private School Association, the Union of Netherlands Municipalities, etc.

The involvement of the provincial authorities mainly takes the form of statutory supervisory and judicial duties. The provincial councils ensure the availability of adequate numbers of publicly run primary and secondary schools and act as appeal bodies with regard to decisions taken by the municipal authorities. With regard to the management of schools and the curriculum, the role of the provinces is limited, partly because they cannot be the competent authority of an educational institution. The municipal authorities have a dual role: they are both the local authority for all schools in the area (whether publicly or privately run) and at the same time the competent authority (school board) for the publicly run schools.

All schools have a legally recognized competent authority, also referred to as its school board. The competent authority administers and manages the school or schools for which it is responsible. It is also responsible for what goes on in the school in so far as this is governed by statutory regulations. The municipality is the competent authority for the publicly run schools in its area. Private schools have as their competent authority the board of an association or foundation set up to provide private education.

Teacher and parent groups, associations of school directors, and trade unions have been influential actors in educational policy-making. These specialists cooperate with government officials in permanent and temporary advisory bodies and provide an important source of technocratic considerations. Experts also reside in research institutes and fact-finding agencies. Research institute personnel are employed by the ministry and these experts are known to move back and forth between the two employers (research institute and government agency).

The school struggle was the core reason for the agreement to cease conflict through a so-called pact for 'pacification' which, by the subsequent establishment of the pillarized system, influenced the shape of Dutch society. It is therefore not surprising that government has always had a strong inclination toward consensus-seeking as well as depolarization of the education sector. The role of technocratic factors in decision-making in the education sector can therefore be expected to have been considerable.

The Emergence and Nature of the Indian Education System

In terms of its historical context, the education system of India owes little to the traditional Hindu or Muslim systems of education that prevailed before the advent of Europeans on the subcontinent. As a matter of fact, the colonial education system was not a modernized transformation of any traditional system of Indian education. It was established outside the traditional systems and without any relationship to them. During British rule, the Charter Act of 1813 had permitted missionaries to go to India in order to educate and proselytize, while the East India Company had accepted responsibility to educate Indians in Western knowledge. In 1823 a General Committee on Public Instruction was set up to give shape to an education policy that the Government of India needed to pursue. This committee consisted of Orientalists and Anglicists, and the ideas of both groups were put before Lord Macaulay who at the time was Law Member of India. Macaulay rejected the ideas of the Orientalists and, through a forceful and now well-known Minute, made a vigorous plea for Western learning taught through the English language.

In 1837 English was made the language of administration, and a government resolution of 1844 threw subordinate positions open to Indians. The result was that institutions of oriental learning declined as English was made the main language of study and the medium of instruction after the primary stage. There was a rapid expansion of schools and colleges that taught English education, with the higher stratum of society adopting and patronizing it. The system of English education had taken root. It was this restrictive system of education that India inherited at the time of Independence. The post-Independence history of reform is related to the manner in which education was sought to be made accessible to all sections of society, and the struggle has been to unshackle the system from its colonial past.

At Independence, therefore, India inherited an education system with little emphasis on literacy or on mass education. Select institutions provided Western education in English, and these were accessible only to the few and the privileged. Consequently, the literacy rate in India was very low: 18.3 per cent overall, with female literacy being only 8.9 per cent. Given this enormous problem, universalization of basic education became the goal of independent India. By 1991, according to census data, the literacy rate had risen to 52.2 per cent. Yet nearly half the population remains illiterate. In 1991 there were more illiterate persons than in 1951. Today the absolute number of illiterates is greater than at the time of Independence.

Furthermore, while there has been tremendous expansion in the number of primary schools, the proportion of children in the 6–14 years age-bracket who remain out of school is high. And among the children who join school, around half of them drop out by the time they reach class eight. The proportion is higher among girls and those who belong to the socially deprived sections of society. There are large numbers of single teacher schools and, indeed, absentee teacher schools. On both demand and supply sides, India has not been able to fulfil the goal laid down in the Constitution of India in 1950.

Aside from low national averages, the educational achievements in India are highly uneven because literacy rates vary a great deal by region, class, caste, and gender. Within a given region, literacy rates are usually lower among those who are economically underprivileged. Literacy rates also tend to be low among Scheduled Castes, Scheduled Tribes, and Muslims. The most worrying part of the situation is the high male–female gap in literacy rates. According to the United Nations Development Programme's *Human Development Report 1998*, only five countries—Bhutan, Syria, Togo, Malawi and, Mozambique—have a higher male–female literacy gap than that of India. One Indian state alone, Rajasthan, has as large a population as all these five countries combined, and no country has a higher male–female literacy gap than Rajasthan.

During the last fifty years, the situation has improved over time but the rate of progress has been slow. As Drèze and Sen (1995: 3) forcefully emphasize,

> the point is not that there has been no progress in India, or that other countries are all doing better, but specifically that India's success in removing poverty, disease, and inequality of opportunity has markedly been less substantial than that of many countries. And in one particular field—that of elementary education—India stands considerably behind even an average of the poor countries of the world.

Article 45 of the Directive Principles of the Constitution of India urges all states to provide 'free and compulsory education for all children until they attain the age of 14 years'—and that goal was originally expected to be reached by 1960. Even at the end of the twentieth century, however, the goal had not been achieved. During the 1990s, the discussion has been to make the right to education justiciable. After considerable delay, 93rd Amendment to the Constitution ensuring Right to Education as a fundamental right was passed by the parliament in 2001. For the first time, however, massive international aid led by the World Bank through its District Primary Education Programme (DPEP) has been accepted. In addition, the government has moved toward supporting voluntary agencies in spreading literacy and making local village communities more responsible for primary education.

EDUCATION COMMISSION 1964

The Education Commission of 1964–6 provided the first comprehensive effort after Independence at reviewing India's educational system. The 1948–9 University Education Commission and the

1952 Secondary Education Commission had respectively looked at university and secondary education in a compartmentalized fashion but, despite extremely low literacy rates in India, no committee or commission had been established for primary and adult education. In addition to its mandate to look comprehensively at education, the 1964 Commission was charged with the responsibility to suggest a national education system for the country. Since the Commission submitted its report in 1966, all subsequent educational policies adopted have been either heavily influenced by its recommendations or designated their departures from it.

In a perceptive analysis of the Commission (Naik 1982), its Member-Secretary suggested that it had raised debates on education that had not occurred earlier because it sharpened reaction to issues that were more political rather than educational in nature. For example, the use of regional languages as the medium of instruction at university level was an issue that raised a storm in political circles. While not the main recommendation of the report, it had been suggested earlier. In fact the 1948–9 University Education Commission, the 1962 Emotional Integration Committee, and the 1962 Vice-Chancellors' Conference had all made the same recommendation. However, the political situation in the late 1960s was such that opposition to this recommendation tended to influence much of the overall reaction to the Education Commission.

In its resolution laying down terms of reference for the Commission, the Government of India emphasized that 'it is desirable to survey the entire field of educational development as the various parts of the education system strongly interact with and influence one another'. It suggested that what 'is needed is a synoptic survey and an imaginative look at education considered as a whole and not fragmented into parts and stages'. It further went on to say that

> while planning of education for India must necessarily emanate from Indian experience and conditions, Government of India are of the opinion that it would be advantageous to draw upon the experience and thinking of educationists and scientists from other parts of the world in the common enterprise of seeking for the right type of education which is the quest of all mankind, specially at this time when the world is getting closely knit together in so many ways.

The United Nations Educational, Scientific and Cultural Organization (UNESCO) provided three international experts on the

Commission. They were Jean Thomas, Inspector General of Education in France and formerly Assistant Director General of UNESCO; Anatoly Shumovsky, Director, Methodological Division, Ministry of Higher and Special Secondary Education in the Russian Soviet Federated Socialist Republic and Professor of Physics at Moscow University; and Sadatoshi Ihara, Professor of the Faculty of Science and Technology at Waseda University, Tokyo. The Government of India also hoped that the collaboration of other eminent scientists and educationists would be available as consultants.

The Commission was headed by Dr D.S. Kothari, Chairman of the University Grants Commission. An eminent scientist and Professor of Physics at Delhi University, he had worked closely with the team that advised Nehru about science matters. Other than the chairman and the three foreign members, there were eleven more members plus a member-secretary. All of them were connected with the profession of education in one way or another. The Member-Secretary was J.P. Naik, Head of the Department of Education Planning, Administration and Finance at Poona's Gokhale Institute of Politics and Economics. Naik had made a name for himself as an educational activist and had established the Indian Institute of Education in Poona. A prolific writer, he was the moving spirit behind the Commission and its recommendations.

In addition there were two foreigners apart from those seconded by UNESCO. H.L. Elvin was Director of the Institute of Education at the University of London and Roger Reville was the Dean of Research at the University of California. Out of 16 members of the Commission, therefore, five were foreigners and represented the educational systems of France, Soviet Russia, Japan, the UK, and the US. All of these countries were in the developed world. There were, however, no experts from countries which were either experimenting with innovative systems or struggling to achieve education for all.

The remaining nine members were also connected with education in one capacity or the other. Among the academic administrators were A.R. Dawood, former Director, Extension Programme for Secondary Education; R.A. Gopalaswami, Director of the Institute of Applied Manpower Research; V.S. Jha, former Director of the Commonwealth Education Liaison Unit in London; P.N. Kirpal, Educational Adviser to the Government of India; K.G. Saiyidain, former Educational Adviser to the Government of India; and B.P.

Pal, Director of the Indian Agricultural Research Institute. Among those connected with universities were M.V. Mathur, Professor of Economics and Public Administration at Rajasthan University; S. Panandiker, Head of the Department of Education, Karnataka University; and Triguna Sen, Rector of Jadavpur University outside Calcutta.

To understand the nature of the recommendations and the working of the Commission, it is necessary to stress that the Commission consisted of people who were intimately involved in the field of education and its administration. Nearly all had some relationship to a university or an institute of higher education. There was a strong bias towards specialization in the fields of science and technology. Another weakness pointed out by Naik himself (1982: 57) was that even though the Commission called its report 'Education and National Development', it had little to say on development or on society. He feels that this happened because there were no social scientists on the Commission. Naik subsequently became founding Member-Secretary of the Indian Council of Social Science Research and believed that no education planning is possible without substantial inputs from the social sciences. One final characteristic of the composition of the Commission was that there was only one woman member.

In the course of its work, the Commission travelled the length and breadth of the country while holding discussions and seminars, visiting schools, colleges, and universities. Two conferences with student representatives were also held. According to the calculation of Commission itself, over 900 persons were interviewed and the total number of notes and memoranda sent to the Commission was around 2,400. About 20 international consultants also met the Commission. These included eminent persons like Professor Edward Shils and Lord Robbins. The Commission set up twelve task forces on (1) school education, (2) higher education, (3) technical education, (4) agricultural education, (5) adult education, (6) science education, (7) teacher training and teacher status, (8) student welfare, (9) new techniques and methods, (10) manpower, (11) educational administration, and (12) educational finance. In addition it set up seven working groups on (1) women's education, (2) education of backward classes, (3) school buildings, (4) school community relations, (5) statistics, (6) pre-primary education, and (7) school curriculum. The task forces and the working groups made a detailed study of the specific problems assigned to them and presented their reports to the Commission.

Each task force or working group included two or three members of the Commission and, on average, consisted of around a dozen members. Many sub-groups were also appointed. The result was that more than 250 experts and educational administrators participated in these deliberations. Agencies like UNESCO and the British Council provided support by supplying international members and consultants. In addition, UNESCO provided the Associate Secretary, Mr McDougall, as well as office support.

The Education Commission submitted its report in June 1966 after a labour of two years. Indira Gandhi had become the prime minister in January 1966 after the death of Lal Bahadur Shastri in whose tenure the Commission had been appointed. But there was some continuity because M.C. Chagla had remained education minister in both cabinets. When the report was submitted, Chagla held a press conference and made its recommendations public for wider discussion and debate. The copy of the report was available in September 1966 and was distributed to the state governments, the Vice-Chancellors' Conference, the Central Advisory Board of Education (CABE), and members of both houses of parliament. The expectation was that, after comments had been received, the Government of India would issue a statement on Education Policy.

However, elections were announced in early 1967 and the processes of consultation continued until a new government under Indira Gandhi came to power in March 1967. The cabinet was changed and Dr Triguna Sen, who was a member of the Commission, took over the portfolio of education. But as Naik (1982: 31) pointed out, Sen—although dedicated to implementation of the report—lacked a political base. He therefore found it difficult to carry the state governments and others with him, particularly when he ceased to command the confidence of the prime minister. Undaunted as well as committed to the report, Sen proceeded to appoint a committee comprised of members of parliament, which represented all the different political parties. He expected that, based on a report of this parliamentary committee, he could prepare a draft for a national policy and place it before parliament.

The new parliamentary committee was asked to (a) consider the Report of the Kothari Commission, (b) prepare a draft statement on the national policy on education, and (c) identify a programme for immediate action. However, discussions in the committee were contentious. The wide differences of opinion can be gauged from the fact that no less than 9 of the 30 members wrote minutes of dissent which ran into 23 pages against a report of 26 pages. The discussions centred around only a few issues that related to 'selectivism' in admissions or in choosing universities for special funding or the medium of instruction. Most other issues were ignored.

Unfazed, the education minister took the report of this parliamentary committee and that of the Commission for discussion to the CABE as well as to the Vice-Chancellors' Conference. While the Board spent most of its time debating the issue of the medium of instruction, the Vice-Chancellors' Conference debated the proposal on choosing major universities for special funding. As a result, the 1968 policy document was a very watered-down version of the Kothari Commission Report. While the recommendations of the Commission were kept alive by subsequent education ministers through assurances of implementation, all of these ministers belonged to the Congress party. But even this pretence was dropped as the country moved to more immediate concerns during the 1970s.

NATIONAL EDUCATION POLICY 1986

The adoption of the 1968 education policy based largely on the recommendations of the Kothari Commission led to considerable expansion in education facilities throughout the country at all levels. Perhaps the most notable development was the acceptance of a common structure of education wherein all the Indian states implemented the 10+2 model for schools and three years for an undergraduate degree. Another significant development was the institutionalization of the leadership role of the Central government. While the Kothari Commission was conducting its deliberations and when the 1968 policy was enunciated, the federal system had specified education as a subject within the sole responsibility of the states. A 1976 constitutional amendment, however, reassigned education to the Concurrent List. This shift had substantive implications because it required that governmental responsibility for education would be shared. It also enjoined the Central government to accept a larger leadership role by providing guidance in innovative programmes and by supporting the states with finance and administration if required by the states for implementing those innovative programmes.

From the time that Rajiv Gandhi took over as Prime Minister on the death of Indira Gandhi, he began to refer to the need for a new education policy. In one of his first radio broadcasts after the assumption of office, he said that our 'educational system needs to be reconstructed as a dynamic force for national growth and integration. I intend to initiate a comprehensive review of the system and to build a national consensus on reform.' Soon after winning a massive mandate in the December 1984 elections, he again referred to education as having a dynamic role to promote national cohesion and the work-ethic. In a speech on 5 January 1985, he proclaimed that 'I have asked that a new national education policy be drafted.' Speaking to the State Education Ministers Conference in August 1985, he not only underlined the need for a new education policy but also raised several questions that needed to be tackled with urgency. These included issues of values, questions of unequal opportunity and gender bias, and the role of education in smoothening social tensions. These issues and questions became the focus of debate and deliberations that followed later. Thus the policy that emerged in 1986 was a product of strong commitment from the Prime Minister himself.

As preparation, two premier institutions—the National Council of Education Research and Training (NCERT) and the National Institute of Education Planning and Administration (NIEPA)—were asked to provide a comprehensive appraisal of the existing educational scene. This appraisal was published by the Government of India in August 1985 as the *Challenge of Education: A Policy Perspective* in order to elicit national debate. Recognizing the contributions of earlier committees and particularly the Kothari Commission, the document laid down its perspective by saying that 'perhaps the problems of today [are] more the result of tardy and haphazard implementation and a progressive decline in the allocation of resources'. It then went on to suggest that the 'new education policy should articulate the educational imperatives not only in terms of objectives, concepts and priorities but it should also spell out an operational strategy with associated financial, material, organizational and human requirements to achieve the long and short objectives laid down in the policy'. It argued that if radical change is accepted in education policy, equally radical instruments and organizational structures would have to be devised to give it a practical shape. This document became the basis for many seminars and workshops while comments were solicited directly from the public. National institutions like NCERT and NIEPA were harnessed to organize these meetings and to sift through the large number of individual comments. Consultations were also held with the CABE.

The National Policy of Education was laid on the table of the parliament in early 1986. The major thrust of its enunciated policy was to develop a strategy of implementation, accompanied by the assignment of specific responsibilities for financial and organizational support. The most urgent tasks that it set itself to tackle were the problems of access, quality, quantity, utility, and financial outlay. It set these problems in the emerging phase of India's social and political life which was increasingly characterized by inequality and the lack of social justice. Speaking to the National Development Council in April 1986, the prime minister said that the idea is not to eliminate or destroy a system that has been in practice. The attempt is to guide the system in particular specific directions and to try to stop its drift. 'The thrust in all this', he continued, 'is to eliminate inequalities, to liberate talents and to achieve a national fulfilment.' The policy document was a brief 29 pages which laid down a strategy of implementation.

While some organizational actions began to be initiated as a consequence of this policy, Rajiv Gandhi and his party lost the electoral mandate in 1989, and a new government led by V.P. Singh came into power. In May 1990, this coalition government appointed a committee to review the 1986 Policy of Education—which was initiated even before the stipulated period of five years had been completed. The urgency reflected the nature of the coalition in power, which had the support of backward and minority communities and had on its agenda a contentious 'reservation' policy recommended by the Mandal Commission. In the announcement of the setting up of the Review Committee, the government provided its perspective when it said:

> Government accords the highest priority to education both as a human right and as the means for bringing about a transformation towards a more humane and enlightened society. There is need to make education an effective instrument for securing a status of equality for women and persons belonging to the backward castes and the minorities. Moreover, it is essential to give work and employment orientation to education and exclude from it the elitist aberrations which have become the glaring

characteristic of the educational scene. Educational institutions are increasingly influenced by casteism, communalism and obscurantism and it is necessary to lay emphasis on struggle against this phenomenon and to move towards a genuinely egalitarian and secular social order. [Therefore] the National Policy on Education 1986 needs to be reviewed to evolve a framework which would enable the country to move towards this perspective of education.

The Review Committee itself pointed out that these concerns were not new but that it intended to give a new direction and to make a break from the past.

To chair the Review Committee, the V.P. Singh government appointed Acharya Ramamurti, a social worker and long-time associate of Jayaprakash Narayan. An Additional Secretary in the Department of Education, Government of India was appointed as Member-Secretary. Other than these two, the committee consisted of 15 members. Most of the members (at least ten of them) were connected with universities or institutions of higher learning. One member was the chair of the National Open School and had been associated in the past with a Christian missionary society working for school education. Another member belonged to the Dayananda Anglo-Vernacular Society concerned with college education. Other three members worked in non-governmental organizations running schools. The committee was heavily loaded towards experience with higher education.

Following the practice of the Kothari Commission, the 1990 Review Committee adopted a procedure of wide-ranging consultations and discussions in order to finalize its recommendations. Six subcommittees were constituted for considering various subjects in detail. These subjects were: (1) access, equity, and universalization; (2) education and the right to work; (3) quality and standards in education; (4) national unity, value education, and character building; (5) resources and management; and (6) rural education. Each subcommittee was authorized to co-opt additional members. While each subcommittee had four or five members, the number of co-opted members and special invitees for their meetings exceeded fifty. The subcommittees held formal discussions with as many people as possible. Some field studies were also conducted and NCERT presented a paper on citizen perceptions of the 1986 policy. Many seminars and workshops were held in various parts of the country.

The Ramamurti Committee submitted its report in December 1990, which was tabled in both houses of parliament on 9 January 1991. At its March 1991 meeting, the CABE considered the procedure to be adopted for consideration of the report and decided that a committee of its own should be constituted by its own Chairman (the Minister of Human Resources Development) for this purpose. It must be pointed out that, by this time, the ministry that had appointed the Acharya Ramamurti Committee had fallen and that a new government headed by P.V. Narasimha Rao had come into power. The government was again one of the Congress party that, under Rajiv Gandhi, had enunciated the 1986 policy.

Following this decision, the minister appointed a committee with sixteen members and chaired by Janardhana Reddy, Chief Minister and Education Minister of Andhra Pradesh. The committee is popularly known by his name. The Joint Secretary in the Department of Education was appointed as Member-Secretary. There were six other ministers from Madhya Pradesh, Arunachal Pradesh, Bihar, Tamil Nadu, West Bengal, and Kerala. The other eight members of the committee consisted of a member of the Planning Commission, chair of the University Grants Commission, a university professor, chair of a development institute (long associated with UNESCO), principal of an innovative school, a scientist, a functionary of a social service organization and, most interestingly, a folk theatre personality. This committee appeared to be the first in which there was a mix of political leaders, experts, and administrators.

The Janardhana Reddy Committee invited comments from the state governments on the Report of the Ramamurti Review Committee and asked the Department of Education to prepare detailed comments on each chapter of the report. Other members of the Advisory Board as well as officials and non-officials commented on the report. All these documents formed the basis for deliberations by the Reddy Committee. Although expected to submit its report within two months after its appointment in July 1991, the committee took much longer and the report was submitted in January 1992. The committee found that, while the concerns of Ramamurti Review Committee were unexceptionable, very few of its recommendations had policy implications. Therefore, it found little ground for revision of the 1986 policy. Nonetheless, it recommended that the plan of action needed to be revised. The next task was to prepare a programme of action in order to revise the 1986 National Education Policy suitably.

In order to draft a Program of Action, a Steering Committee consisting of fourteen members was established. Chaired by a member of the Planning Commission, this committee was comprised mostly of government functionaries like the University Grants Commission Chair and Secretaries to the Government. Twenty-two task forces comprising educationists as well as officials of state and Central governments were constituted on different subjects. The twenty-two subject areas were: (1) education for women's equality, (2) education of Scheduled Castes, Scheduled Tribes, and other weaker sections, (3) minorities' education, (4) education of the handicapped, (5) adult and continuing education, (6) early childhood care and education, (7) elementary education, (8) secondary education, (9) *Navodaya Vidyalayas*, (10) vocational education, (11) higher education, (12) open education, (13) rural universities/institutes, (14) technical and management education, (15) research and development, (16) media and educational technology, (17) delinking degrees from jobs and manpower planning, (18) cultural perspective and development of languages, (19) sports, physical education, and youth, (20) evaluation and examination, (21) teachers and their training, and (22) management of education. Many of the task forces included members of the Steering Committee but also at least 250 other experts and administrators. The task force reports were included as a chapter of the document. As the draft report was oriented towards implementation, it was first discussed at a conference of State Secretaries and Directors of Education. After incorporating the suggestions made at that conference, a draft 'Program of Action' was placed before the CABE which, after due consideration, endorsed the document in 1992.

A follow-up to the 1992 'Program of Action' was further deliberation on decentralized management of education. Two constitutional amendments (73rd and 74th) had been adopted that placed the institutions of Panchayati Raj and urban governance on a constitutional footing. Education was among the subjects included within the jurisdiction of panchayats and municipalities, and the state legislatures were expected to make suitable laws in this regard. The 'Program of Action' had recommended that a CABE committee be set up to prepare guidelines on decentralized management of education in the light of these amendments. Set up in 1993 and chaired by the Chief Minister of Karnataka, CABE approved its committee's report in the same year. Technical assistance for this committee was provided by NIEPA.

One characteristic feature of policy-making in education is India's federal system and the fact that education was initially included in the list of subjects reserved for the states. Only in 1974 through a constitutional amendment did education become part of the Concurrent List which signified that both the Centre and the states could legislate in the field. Even after this amendment, however, the Centre never took unilateral decisions but rather undertook elaborate consultative processes before formulating any policy. In most cases, it developed guidelines and then through wide-ranging discussions cajoled the states to implement them. When necessary, the Centre provided funds to implement the schemes that it suggested.

Both policy as well as implementation processes are time consuming and always involve delay as well as require patience. Much of this central funding comes as a plan expenditure so, when the plan completes its five year cycle, the responsibility for sustaining such schemes falls on the state governments. By accepting a central scheme and its money, states postpone their direct responsibility until the post-plan period. Some states hesitate to undertake such delayed responsibility or else fulfil their parts of the bargain inadequately. This situation is not conducive for full commitment to any scheme or policy, and state acceptance of Central initiatives may only reflect the lure of extra funds. Many schemes that followed from the New Education Policy of 1986—like Operation Blackboard or District Institutes of Education and Training (DIET)—have reflected this hesitation when being implemented. The probability of under-implementation leads to the need for continuous monitoring by Central agencies over the performance of their schemes as well as maintenance of dialogue with state implementing agencies. A vast network of committees and visiting teams has thus appeared in order to oversee implementation of education projects. The Education Ministry of the Government of India finds itself drowned in problems of implementation without having the direct ability to resolve them.

In many cases this process becomes quite contentious and appeals involve the political level. Hence conferences of chief ministers and education ministers are frequently held in order to iron out differences or to legitimize the proposals of the Centre. The issue of making the right to free and compulsory education a Fundamental Right and to enforce it through suitable statutory measures is a case in point. After consultations with technical experts were exhausted, the proposal was discussed at a Conference of Chief Ministers on 4–5 July 1996 and then at a Conference of Education Ministers on 10 August 1996. The issue figured again in a meeting of experts with the education minister and then the decision was taken to appoint a Committee of State Education Ministers in order to consider the financial, administrative, legal, and academic implications of the proposal. This subcommittee submitted its report in January 1997. Subsequently, the political configuration of the government changed and little has been heard of the proposal since then.

On a regular basis the CABE meets which is chaired by the Government of India's minister of education and its members are the state education ministers. Among nominated members of this Board are state-level administrators and other experts. The education ministry seeks advice from this Board on all matters that concern the states. The Board also establishes its own subcommittees to examine issues in depth such as the case of decentralized management of education.

The education ministry draws on the expertise available at NCERT and NIEPA for advice on routine operational and policy issues. This advisory support is widened by involving others from different institutions in the country whenever wider consultation and discussions are needed. As voluntary groups have become more involved in primary education and literacy programmes in recent years, their representation in the consultative process is also visible. While the Central government tends to involve the state governments more in the policy planning process, the Education Department has lagged behind in consulting horizontally with other related Central departments like those of social welfare or tribal development. This has sometimes resulted in duplication of programmes and lack of coordination.

To summarize, even though a nationwide review of education policy had been considered by Nehru, it was his successor as Prime Minister, Lal Bahadur Shastri, who appointed an Education Commission chaired by Dr D.S. Kothari. By the time the Commission presented its report, Indira Gandhi had become prime minister and was fighting for her political survival in both party and government. Education not being among her priorities, she left it to her Education Minister, Dr Triguna Sen, to steer the report through parliament. Although Triguna Sen was well intended and sincerely supported the work of the Commission, he knew little about education and even less about primary education; and because Mrs Gandhi lacked extensive political support, it was necessary to create a political consensus. Some sort of consensus did emerge but, in the process, controversies were created over some recommendations.

Consequently the 1968 National Education Policy was largely anodyne with few actions undertaken to ensure that the recommendations were implemented. Until 1986 when a new education policy was devised, only a few of the Kothari Commission's recommendations bore fruit. The new education policy was designed at the insistence of Rajiv Gandhi, by then prime minister, who was notably impatient. Although his civil service and political advisors counselled caution and advised widespread consultations to build consensus, the 1986 policy was hurriedly formulated due to the personal involvement of the prime minister. At least unlike earlier education policies, issues of implementation were not neglected and a 'Program of Action' was prepared. The leadership of the prime minister, plus the fact that a 'Program of Action' was prepared at the outset, helped lay the policy on the ground fairly quickly. This was in contrast to the 1968 policy that had a much larger gestation period. It took more than two decades, for example, for the national education system of 10+2 for school and three years of under-graduate studies to become established.

The policy process described above conforms with the general perception that educational decisions in India are political decisions and rarely reflect technical expertise in education. The political economy of education has remained a dominating factor in determining educational programmes. Reports of expert committees and even those of this Commission were processed by political leadership and made available for public debate. If the problem lies in the state arena, state political leaders are consulted on a formal basis. Consequently, while there is undoubtedly a gain in political legitimacy, recommendations are considerably watered-down (if not altogether rejected), and considerable delay occurs before a policy document emerges from such deliberations. Many recommendations continue to linger, get included in other reports or become debating points to be used for political advantage.

Despite the exception of several notable politicians, education has not been on the agenda of India's political parties. They have not focused on educational problems as technical problems but have been more concerned with the political consequences of educational issues. Little time is spent for in-depth analysis of problems or for understanding them. However, although political initiatives are rare, there is considerable reluctance to leave things to the experts. The result is that a hiatus between politicians and experts has grown into negative mutual perceptions. More often than not, educational propositions are turned into grist for the political mill from which emanates ultimate power. From the way state ministers are assigned the education portfolio, political parties do not consider it of great significance. Usually the weakest among the ministers is given responsibility for education. At the central level the record has been no different. In the last two decades, education has gone to political light-weights, or to those who have no interest in education other than using it to advance their own political fortunes in other fields.

A widely shared view is that education is fit only for academics and that politicians should keep their hands off it. When the Education Commission was appointed in 1964, the Union Education Minister M.C. Chagla boasted that he had not appointed any politician to it. But such splendid isolation made educationists blind to many aspects of educational reality which are basically political. As Naik (1982: 197) argues, an issue like that of selective admissions cannot be solved except jointly by politicians and educationists. On the other hand, because of this very isolation, the politicians remain largely ignorant of basic educational problems so that when they interfere with education—which they often do—they do more harm than good. In other words, the educationists desire full political support without any political interference (which is their concept of autonomy) while politicians interfere too frequently with education (which is their concept of accountability to the legislature) without committing themselves to provide any support.

Chapter 6

Dynamics of Advisory Commissions: Comparative Features

THE DIFFERENCES IN trends between the Netherlands and India described in the two previous chapters would suggest little likelihood of finding common features in the functioning of advisory committees. Whereas the Dutch have a tradition of depoliticization, which adds to the influence of technocratic decision-making, the Indian decision-making process is highly politicized which thereby counters the influence of technocrats. Quite unexpectedly, however, many common features were identified in different stages of a committee's existence, from the moment of its establishment until the point of committee follow up. The similarity in nature and procedures of the committees in both countries also enables the researcher to analyse their differences. Comparisons of these similarities and differences suggest that Dutch and Indian decision-making processes share more traits than one might initially expect.

The validation of information reported below is complicated by the ethics of confidentiality. While approximately sixty respondents kindly consented to be interviewed during the study, they did so on the agreement that direct citations would not be made. The Appendix 1 lists eight Dutch committees on health and education issues, and some members of each were interviewed. Likewise, selected members of health and education commissions in India shared their views, but again on the promise of personal confidentiality. Hence the information can only be reported in generalizable terms with occasional vignettes from unattributed sources.

MECHANICS OF COMMITTEES

Most committees deal with money or, more specifically, with obtaining value for money through organizational and occasionally systemic reforms. In the Netherlands, the search for efficiency and effectiveness in the provision of health care and educational services has been the main drive for establishing temporary advisory committees. In some cases, parts of the service delivery system were perceived as being too expensive (van Eijndhoven, de Jager); sometimes a complete system reform was the final objective (Dekker, Dunning, Stekelenburg). In three cases, committees were established in order to gain time during stressful or conflictful periods (Biesheuvel, Bruins-Slot, Welschen). Two committees (Stekelenburg, de Jager) officially were restricted to evaluatory activities but were requested to formulate recommendations for future improvements too. One respondent even alleged a hidden agenda behind the establishment of the Dunning Committee, namely to prove the impossibility of limiting the costs of health care. He hypothesized that, if outstanding professionals were unable to devise feasible propositions for cost control, then nobody else could be expected to do so either.

In India, on the other hand, while concern for public resources (particularly their scarcity) was never absent, temporary advisory commissions and committees were largely motivated by issues of equity or, more accurately, of inequity. From the 1943 Bhore Committee through the 1981 ICSSR/ICMR joint committee, the quest for equitable, effective, and efficient health care dominated deliberations—although a number of intervening commissions addressed organizational mechanisms and personnel arrangements to attain this overall goal. In the field of education, the Kothari Commission reviewed the entire system in order to recommend ways in which to provide schooling for the masses without undermining higher education which was already imparting relatively high quality skills. The stimulus behind the multiple consultations that led up to, and then followed, the 1986 National Education Policy was the urge to deliver educational services that had so often been promised.

In the Netherlands, most initiatives to establish a committee come from a primary political official—usually the (deputy) minister—in close cooperation with senior departmental bureaucrats. These actors also determine the mandate and terms of reference. In some cases, the initiative stems from personal advisors or friends of the (deputy) minister, who then take part in the committee to be formed. Sometimes, parliament compels ministries to establish a committee (Dekker, van Eijndhoven). In one particular case, a new deputy minister was forced to establish the Rispens Committee because of a promise made by her predecessor. In India, a similar pattern applies in that the source of most initiatives lies with the relevant minister, but an exception occurred in 1986 when the initiative for a new education commission came from the prime minister.

In the Netherlands, while the (deputy) minister appoints the members, senior bureaucrats were almost always involved in the selection procedure. The chair is usually selected first, a choice which influences the selection of other committee members. Dunning, Biesheuvel, and van Steekelenburg were said to be very influential in this respect. Committee members who are personal friends of the (deputy) minister are often involved in the selection of their colleagues too.

The criteria for selection differ, depending on the nature of the committee. Though most health committees were dominated by medical specialists and education committees by experts in the field of education, quite a few of the health committees had a considerable representation of economists (Biesheuvel, Dekker, Welschen). Most committees contained a mixture of insiders (who knew the field) and outsiders (for a fresh look at that field). However, known adversaries of intended governmental policies are never appointed to a committee. Public recognition was also an important factor. The chairperson invariably had an impeccable reputation and brought considerable visibility to the committee (Dekker, Biesheuvel). The chair was often an outsider to the field, too, and therefore likely to be regarded as impartial (Dekker, Biesheuvel, Bruins-Slot, Welschen).

In the 'crisis' committees, prior affiliation of members is an important criterion. The affiliation can be with political parties or interest groups in the field. The importance of political party affiliation in the selection phase, however, does not guarantee political battles in the committees. Most respondents in the Netherlands claimed that party affiliation did not dominate the debate. The Welschen Committee is the only one in which affiliation with one of the two contesting departments became an issue. In India, even though the Indian policy process is highly politicized in terms of pronouncements and criticism, the members of advisory committees are almost always only experts. The education minister in 1964, himself formerly in the judicial branch, took pride over the fact that no politician was appointed on the Education Commission.

In both the field of health and education, committees in India have rarely included economists or social scientists whereas such appointments are relatively common in the Netherlands.

The workload of a committee naturally depends on its mandate. Most Dutch respondents mentioned that they had to work hard and were almost always under time constraints. While 'grand scheme' committees (Dekker, Dunning, Stekelenburg) worked for one to two years, the urgent political committees operated only for six months or thereabouts. In one case (Biesheuvel), the deputy minister sought a pre-advice on part of the workload because of its political urgency, but the committee refused.

Most committees had an explicit division of tasks. Committee members were often selected on the basis of their specific expertize and requested to direct their attention to that specific field. Members sometimes had a pet subject about which he or she would write a chapter. The task division was extremely clear in the Stekelenburg Committee, in which each member wrote a chapter, the four chapters being (later) more or less merged into a complete set of recommendations. The Biesheuvel and the Dunning Committees formed subgroups. In some committees (Rispens, de Jager, van Eijndhoven) a few members did most of the work, but the fruits of their efforts were always discussed in plenary session by all members. Chairpersons usually were good debaters and organizers, who managed the public presentation of the committee reports.

In their deliberations, Dutch committees use data from the ministry or semi-government bodies such as the National Health Council. These data are usually collected by the secretariat and the professional advisors although sometimes an expert committee member collects the relevant data on his/her special field. In most cases, additional studies were needed. These were done by the secretariat (Rispens), by committee members (Dekker, Bruins-Slot, Welschen, de Jager, van Eijndhoven, Stekelenburg), or by external consultants (Biesheuvel, Dunning). The secretariat of the Rispens Committee was contracted out to a private bureau, which also conducted the necessary research. In some cases, the information gaps were only indicated, not filled, because of the limited amount of time. Hearings are used to gather data, too, although there is some question about the direction in which such information flows. Reports of other temporary committees were never mentioned as an important source of information.

The data on which Indian policy-makers based their decisions are generally believed to be unreliable. One respondent noted that 'data on health are almost bogus' while another asserted that the 1985 *Challenge of Education* document was not based on valid data because these contained so many errors. According to yet another respondent, India is in need of a system for collecting information or data on both the providers and seekers of health services. Others, however, suggest that such a major investment in data collection may not have any effect because information is never fully utilized even when available. An example was given of the 1986 Education Policy that had an impressive database on which to build, but the policy draft did not take notice of the public comments that had been made in the wider debate. To the frustration of the experts, the politicians formulated their own views. The information-base was shortlived since old style policy-making had made a return.

Another factor that limits the influence of information is the often mentioned Indian tendency to do what others (read: donors) say rather than to base their action on empirical evidence. Only one respondent claimed that the quality and quantity of educational data have been improving; but, when pressed for examples, he could provide only one source of secure empirical information.

In most cases, the professional advisors or the secretariat wrote the draft and/or final reports. In the Welschen Committee, the professional advisors used this opportunity to influence the outcome of the debate between the two ministries. The secretary of the Rispens Committee and the secretariat of the Biesheuvel Committee wrote all drafts as well as the final report. The professional advisor of the van Eijndhoven committee wrote the draft reports, the chairman wrote the final report. Likewise, in the Dunning Committee, the draft and final reports were written by the secretaries but the summary of the recommendations, which is the most important part, was written by the chairman. In the Bruins-Slot and de Jager Committees, a few expert members wrote the reports. For the Stekelenburg Committee, each expert wrote a separate report, the four of which were later integrated.

In India, the Kothari Commission had a well-known and powerful Member-Secretary J.P. Naik, who is credited with having written the report. His influence during deliberations of the Commission was enormous and he was able to incorporate many of his own ideas into the final product. The document *Challenge to Education*, on which the new policy was based, was written by the bureaucrats within the ministry.

Functions of Committees

Chapter 2 suggested that the establishment of committees coincides with a political inclination toward non-decision-making and, within a longer term perspective, toward maximizing consensus. Temporary committees provide opportunities to postpone a difficult decision, to depoliticize an awkward dispute by technical arguments, and/or to remove the responsibility from government to the temporary body. While some of the committees had such a 'refrigerator-component', others clearly did not. The first so-called 'cooling off' committees were established in situations of political stress and served to give the department some additional time for manoeuvre. These committees deal with highly charged issues in the public arena that politicians and bureaucrats alone could not solve. The second type of committee deals with longer term, substantive policy issues in the bureaucratic arena. These committees usually have more time to research policy options and to deal with issues without political urgency.

The committees selected for investigation in both India and the Netherlands are similar in that they expressly address questions of quality and efficiency in health and education policy. Because ministries responsible for these human capital services are continuously engaged in efforts to economize and to cope with financial constraints, the cost-saving aspect is always present—even though most committees had quality improvement as their official and principle mandate. In some cases, committees produced recommendations that would increase rather than curtail costs, but such exceptions were rare.

The Indian inclination to non-decision-making equals that of the Dutch. The Indian policymaker is primarily preoccupied with the formulation of a new policy, not with its implementation. The purpose usually is to set a perspective—a long-term direction. Rarely does a committee establish goals that can be implemented during the lifetime of the government in power. Value issues are debated and discussed, and the recommendation of the committee is the agreement that emerges among the members of the committee. The establishment of a committee at least suggests to the general public that something is being done. Rather regularly, however, policy advice is not followed by implementation but by a request for new advice which necessitates the establishment of new committees. The Indian committees serve all kinds of purposes: to buy time, to incorporate critics, to obstruct unwelcome policies, and to produce documents from which to quote in the next round of committees.

Committee Procedures

Both in India and the Netherlands, the initiative for the establishment of committees stems from (deputy) ministers in close cooperation of senior bureaucrats. These are also responsible for the formulation of the terms of reference, and the selection of the committee members. In the Netherlands, the chairman sometimes has a say about the terms of reference and the composition of the committees, but always in close cooperation with the concerned department. The Indian process appears to be more overly political. The terms of reference are kept at a general level, thus allowing the committee to move in the way desired by the chairperson or member-secretary. As concrete implementable suggestions are not expected, the process allows bureaucrats to set up further committees to process the suggestions for implementation. It is for this reason that the committee process is a long, winding, time-consuming one. With constitutional responsibility for both education and health assigned to the state arena, the federal system requires consultation between two levels of government before decisions can be taken for implementation.

The criteria for selection of committee members vary, depending on the nature of the committee. In general, three different kinds of specialists are selected: content or substance experts (professionals in health or education), financial experts (economists and businessmen), and process or procedural experts (managers, administrators, and lawyers). Financial professionals were in committees on both education and health care. Their appearance indicates the importance of issues of efficiency in Dutch decision-making. The procedural experts include the chairpersons and retired politicians. Most committees contain a mixture of insiders (who knew the field) and outsiders (for a fresh look on that field). In India, most committees consist of substantive specialists in the particular policy sector.

The voluntary sector has increasingly been consulted when determining policies during the last two decades. The committee to review Indian Education Policy in 1990 was headed by a person belonging to this sector. The VHAI has also played a greater role in interacting with government over policy issues. What is significant is that the private sector, which is increasing its presence in the two domains of education and health delivery, has not gained adequate recognition for participation in the deliberation of such communities.

In both countries, a committee's chair has to have nearly impeccable standing and be able to bring visibility to the committee. In the Netherlands the chairperson often is an outsider to the field and therefore likely to be impartial. In India, on the other hand, the impartiality of the chairman is assured by his standing in the field of expertise. The appointment of a secretary or member-secretary is also critical. To a great extent this focal official determines the kind of background work that needs to be done in order to provide a basis for discussions. The secretary is instrumental in searching for relevant documents and for identifying experts or knowledgeable persons who may be invited before the committee for consultation. Often the secretary assigns research tasks to outside individuals or agencies. He/she also often writes the interim and final reports.

Both in India and the Netherlands, known adversaries of intended government policies are never requested to join a committee. In 'crisis prevention' committees in the Netherlands, party affiliation is an important criterion. The affiliation can be with political parties *per se* or with interest groups in the field. The importance of political party affiliation in the selection phase does not guarantee political battles during committee deliberations. Most respondents claimed that party affiliation did not dominate the debate. There have been no similar 'crisis committees' in India. As a respondent mentioned, demands for new policies in health and education have emerged from the perceptions of needs by the leadership.

The expertize of the Dutch committee-members often matches the specializations of the professional observers from the ministry. Because these observers officially are not allowed to influence the debate, there was little evidence of professional loyalties or coalitions between the members and the observers. However, the data on the basis of which committees have to formulate their proposals usually come from the department or from semi-governmental research institutes. In both countries, additional research is sometimes undertaken.

In India, the style of policy formulation involves more extensive consultation of and advice from stakeholders than in the Netherlands. An outstanding feature of Indian policy-making is its almost ceaseless efforts toward accommodation and settlement among political, administrative, and specialist groups. For example, in order to determine the 1986 Education Policy, extensive consultations took place as the government sought to reach all levels of expertise and interests through numerous seminars held throughout the country. The purpose was to elicit opinions from as many diverse people as possible; for this, one unusual method employed was to encourage ordinary members of the public to submit their suggestions for reform, even if by postcard. Consequently, thousands of such letters were received and their contents analysed. The Health Policy Statement of 1982 was also a product of such widespread consultations in which a variety of experts—doctors, medical administrators, researchers—from Central and state governments, medical colleges, and research institutions were involved through subcommittees and working groups. It is often argued, however, that these consultative sessions have negligible impact on the content of the final proposal other than, of course, to legitimize the policy through such demonstrably democratic processes.

In the Netherlands, committees usually work in relative isolation from the outside world. Once the committees have drafted their reports, however, meetings and informational sessions are often then organized. These serve to present and gain support for the committee views, not to generate data about the views and demands of the stakeholders. There are, of course, exceptions to this practice which resemble the Indian pattern.

Committees in Operation

INTERNAL FEATURES

Committees are comprised of individuals who represent different interests, different ideological and political parties, and—of particular interest for this study—different professions. The relevance of each of these different factors for the process and the outcome of the debate needs to be distinguished.

The first surprising observation is that most committees were found to operate in harmony. It is surprising in view of the different interests at stake as well as the different affiliations, specializations, and egos of the committee members. Several reasons for this unexpected harmony can be deduced from the answers of our respondents:

- Known adversaries of intended government policies are not invited to join the committee. The selected committee members consequently share a set of basic opinions and preferences. In the Netherlands, political preference appears to be more important as a selection criterion than specific expertise, whereas in India the primary criterion is substantive knowledge of the policy field.
- Despite the political appointments, party politics (as far as we were told) did not dominate Dutch committee debates nor did affiliations with stakeholders in the field. Socially desirable answers should not be accepted uncritically, but the answers unanimously suggest that the committee members (perhaps because of professional ethics) try to keep the debate 'clean'.
- The fact that most chairmen were either outsiders, or politically neutral, was often mentioned as an advantage. The chairmen prevented crises from breaking out and managed to limit the influence of the vested interests. One Dutch committee appointed an external advisor as a secretary, which worked remarkably well. When asked, members of other Dutch committees said that they would have welcomed this arrangement.
- In some committees, members kept mainly (or only) to his/her expertise and did not participate in the debate on the general outline of the report. These reports came out as a collection of individual contributions. Such an arrangement is certain to prevent conflict because all viewpoints are presented, but at a potential loss of overall consistency or coherency.

The lack of emotional struggles over the often sensitive subjects suggests that committees succeeded in depoliticizing the debate through the use of technical arguments. Although respondents sometimes disagreed on the degree of influence of political considerations on the debates, the general opinion was that technical arguments prevailed. Most respondents supported the view that technical arguments were used to keep the debate clean, but some asserted that technical arguments were used for political purposes.

Several respondents suggested that technical arguments mainly serve to give a scientific flavour to political games of interest representation. The political game prevails in the committees and the depoliticization process depends on the traditional bargaining process between the representatives from the middle field rather than from the use of technical arguments, although the latter can help in winning the argument. A similar experience was mentioned by an Indian respondent who wanted to clothe his political argument by raising technical arguments and by requesting more analytical data, but he noted that others had discouraged him from doing so. In the committees, most discussion is based on personal experiences and individual perceptions of the problems.

Opinions on the influence of professional loyalties differ. Respondents who believe in the technical nature of temporary advisory committees point to the existence of professional loyalties rather than to the possible existence of stakeholder-affiliations. Committee members with the same expertize have been reported to work together on data collection and analysis. According to others, professional loyalty is much less important than professional interests. Scientists, they claim, very rarely represent only the scientific interest; they usually represent also the corporate interests.

In the Netherlands, education committees are usually too small to allow groups of members who share the same expertize. Each specific professional field is usually represented by only one individual. The Stekelenburg Committee supports this statement for it contained four educationalists, but each with a different specialization. Each worked on his/her own field without much interaction with one another. Health committees tend to be somewhat larger and are usually dominated by health professionals. In most committees, health professionals from the field met health professionals from the ministry (the professional observers). According to one Dutch respondent, this dominance explains the paternalistic tone of most committee reports. Professional loyalty here is related to interests at stake, the interests of the providers being overrepresented. The representation of all stakeholders in committees make revolutionary proposals highly unlikely, but an all-inclusive practice increases the feasibility and therefore the relevance of the proposals. As another Dutch respondent observed, committees consisting of 'pure' scientists tend to produce brilliant but useless analyses and recommendations.

Because they usually hail from the relevant department or ministry, committee secretaries tend to side with the department's (or minister's) view. In one case the secretary was appointed from outside. External chairpersons and secretaries can be useful because, not being closely connected to the ministry or other stakeholders, they can operate more freely which, in turn, makes it easier to reach agreements. The relative independence of outside advisors/secretaries/chairs sometimes makes departments decide to involve the outside agency in the implementation process. If this process takes a long time (which it usually does), the external advisor builds more knowledge and experience on the case than his/her counterpart from the ministry. This means that a considerable part of the continuity of the policy-making process depends on actors outside the ministry.

The external secretary becomes an extra stakeholder with a separate motivation: the reputation of the bureau or consultancy to which he/she belongs. One respondent, for example, described how he used considerable time and energy to keep the (now unwilling) department interested in the follow-up stage of a particular education project. It is highly unlikely that a regular secretary, without commercial interests, would have worried as much about his name and reputation. Without such commercial motivation, the initiative would long ago have been stopped. It is important, therefore, not to idealize the technocratic nature of professional advice. Health and education policy professionals are rarely value-free. For example, the different intellectual movements within the science of special education are based more on ideology than on empiricism.

EXTERNAL ENVIRONMENT

Unsurprisingly, departments usually try to influence direction of the debates (Dekker, Bruins-Slot, Welschen). Respondents from the Dunning Committee were not unequivocal about the role of the health department. One asserted that the health bureaucrats were stopped by Dunning; another stated that they seriously influenced (and limited) the freedom of debate. Dunning did write a report that was completely in correspondence with government plans. The de Jager Committee was said to remain free of departmental interference. But the independent secretary of the Rispens Committee was nonetheless closely linked to the department. And Stekelenburg himself was part of the Inspectorate which officially is independent but, in practice, operates in co-ordination with the Education Department.

Although the appointments were often political in nature and the political parties tried to influence their representatives in the committees, the respondents gave the impression that they operated rather independently from their parties. While the van Eijndhoven Committee was in operation, the Labor Party's fraction leader (Wallage) introduced a policy motion that called for support for the plans of the committee. This motion was passed which created an enormous amount of support for the committee and the deputy minister.

Some committees deliberately worked in isolation (van Eijndhoven, de Jager). Pressure by the stakeholders from the field on the Dekker Committee was always high, but peaked after the debates on the published report. However, the committee members did not give the impression of having been influenced by the pressure groups during the writing of their report. The hearings that were organized by some (Biesheuvel, Dunning, Welschen) committees did not influence the nature of the committee debates. Most committee members brought in their own expertise and knew what they wanted.

In the Netherlands, refrigerator committees are more common in the health care sector than in education. Since government began its attempts to reform the Dutch health care system in the 1980s, the need for such committees has increased. The 'refrigerator' committees that were studied have been successful in the sense that they did what they were intended to do: preventing a crisis from breaking out and gaining time for the politicians and bureaucrats. In view of this obvious rationale for the establishment of the crisis-prevention committees, it is remarkable how readily the stakeholders accept the committees and thereby let the politicians and bureaucrats get off the hook (as it were). Possible explanations for their cooperation, if not docility, include:

- Stakeholders are not as worried as they claim to be. The display of frustration and disagreement may well be a part of the bargaining game in order to increase the possibility that the committee will take one's interests into account.
- The medical lobby is declining in strength because the peak organization of medical specialists is not as unified as it used to be. Specialization has taken its toll by dividing the medical lobby

among its members. Their negotiating position is weakened by the fact that it is increasingly unclear who the professional provider representatives actually represent.

- Stakeholders rely on the fact that committee reports rarely contain elaborate implementation sections. The implementation phase, if it were ever taken seriously, might be a much more effective arena for lobbying activities.
- Stakeholders do not escape the 'Dutch disease' of instinctive compromise. They are not inclined to spoil a good working relationship with government representatives with whom they may well have to deal in the future. Hardliners are not appreciated in the Dutch constellation of political style.
- Interest groups sometimes act in order to satisfy their constituencies through public visibility. As their *raison d'être* may be at risk, the act of protest in these cases is more important than the results. This observations would rarely apply to service providers, but it chacterizes the operation of many consumer groups.

In India, during the period of our study, the motivation to form committees did not emerge from any impending political crisis. As a matter of fact, the Government of India has not felt the urgency expressed in various committee reports nor show any seriousness by monitoring their implementation. The 1986 New Education Policy emerged through the active initiatives of then Prime Minister Rajiv Gandhi. His initiative went to the extent of sitting with the bureaucrats to identify the major areas of concern and then personally monitoring the formulation of the policy statement. The 1983 'Health for All' policy statement was greatly influenced by the international concern expressed in the Alma Ata Declaration. Both Indian and Dutch stakeholders are often represented in the temporary advisory committees. The fact that the stakeholders do not appear to use the possibility of instructing their representatives to influence the committee debates suggests that they are not overly worried about committee outcomes or their consequences. Affiliated committee members do not consult their rank and file on a regular basis but, when they do, they claim that such consultation does not influence the committee debates.

Our research has found evidence for each of the above-mentioned explanations. In addition, a sixth explanation of stakeholder behaviour emerged: anticipatory behaviour. Okma (1997) describes how most Dutch stakeholders, by means of their peak organizations, while officially objecting to the proposals of the Dekker Committee, individually and secretly developed strategic market behaviour in order to be prepared for the proposed structure. In the case of the Dekker proposals, the stakeholders moved strategically because they started to see advantages in the proposals that they had at first rejected. The official resistance gave them time to change. Another clear example of anticipatory behaviour surfaced in the Dutch education sector.

On the basis of ideological and practical motivations the Rispens Committee proposed to shift the responsibility for the choice between special and normal education from the providers to the parents. The deputy minister had a personal interest in this field, and advocated integration of handicapped pupils into the regular school system. Fearing that they might lose part of their professional autonomy to parent and government organizations, the providers of special education advised against these plans. When the minister installed a committee to investigate the possibilities and their practical implications, the providers fiercely opposed it, and opposition remained present during and after the work of the committee. In the meantime, the providers worked hard to solve the problems that had initially formed the basis for ministerial concerns (lack of expertize in special schools, insufficiently trained personnel, small and inefficient units) and thus removed the practical need for changes. The long process that followed the committee report (and the prolonged period of cabinet-formation) gave the providers the time they needed. The ideological motivation (integration of the handicapped) proved to be an insufficient base to withstand provider-lobbying within the department. The arrival of a new minister and subsequent personnel changes in the ministry meant victory for the providers.

The committee unintentionally supplied the providers with an incentive to effect improvements in their organization as well as in the quality of their product. The sector of special education had long been inefficient (and partially ineffective) but without any incentives for change. The establishment of the Rispens Committee was the first serious threat to the sector, and it motivated the producers to undertake actions they had been reluctant to consider earlier. These improvements directly increased the quality of special education, hence fulfilling a major goal of the primary education directorate.

The composition of the group of stakeholders in India resembles that of the Dutch constellation: government bureaucrats and politicians at national, state, and district level; semi-government research institutes; apex organization of health professionals and teachers; labour unions; pharmaceutical industry; client organizations; external donor organizations. The interviews, however, suggest that they are less organized than their Dutch counterparts. Being less able to confront the powerful bureaucracy, they are forced to accept the committees. Or perhaps they don't bother because the implementation of plans in India is regularly neglected, so stakeholders know how to accommodate [in other words, manipulate] the actions of bureaucrats when necessary.

One set of stakeholders in the Indian setting is almost entirely absent in the Netherlands: international organizations. Although the influence of the European Commission is growing, the impact of international organizations on Dutch policy-making in health and education is negligible. The Indian situation, in which international organizations are important stakeholders, is quite different. Both in health and education, international donor organizations such as the World Health Organization (WHO), United Nations Children's Fund (UNICEF), United Nations Education, Scientific and Cultural Organization (UNESCO), and the United Nations Development Programme (UNDP) seek to influence the content of policy debates. These international pressures are hard to resist. The UNICEF and WHO compare results between countries, which try hard to do well in the 'world sweepstakes'. Health policy is greatly influenced by WHO and international pressures. The latter, for example, continuously stress (and provide the lure of finance for) birth control and AIDS prevention while other more pervasive communicable diseases are neglected. At the Centre, the World Bank is also a major player.

Some Indian respondents questioned the relevance of international influence. It was noted, for example, that the 1983 National Health Policy had allegedly come into existence largely due to external influences like the 1978 Alma Ata Declaration of 'Health for All by the Year 2000', but India had already conceptualized the idea of health for all in the Bhore Report of 1943. The real struggle concerned implementation. Instead of focusing on these implementation problems, however, the Indian government started reformulating and repackaging ideas it already had. As one respondent wryly observed: 'Where money comes, people follow. Policy experts know that integrated policy is best and propose it, but international donors say vertical programs are best—and the Government of India always changes to fit the international flow of money.' According to another, India's problem is that it always follows others; it tries to be 'carbon copies' of arrangements/models elsewhere rather than examining possibilities on the ground.

Indian respondents identified the following groups of stakeholders: government bureaucrats and politicians at national, state, and local levels; semi-governmental research institutes; labour unions; apex organizations of health professionals and teachers; the pharmaceutical industry; diverse client organizations; and external donor organizations. The widely shared opinion is that organizations of clients and consumers are relatively powerless: 'The public is relevant only in the political game in mobilizing micro-level activities.'

Only one respondent asserted that, despite their number, health practitioners and hospitals do not work as a group nor lobby together. According to others, however, they do work as a group, just like their equivalents in education. The general opinion is that the apex organizations of teachers, and health practitioners, are not concerned with issues of quality, but only with wages and salaries. They function as labour unions and do not discuss the quality of the provided services nor related substantial issues. 'Professional associations have no say in politics; nobody wants to change anything.' 'The last 15 years have seen significant inputs and impact from two professional associations: one of elementary teachers, and one of secondary teachers. These not only act as labor unions but also set professional standards and argue for universal values.'

The general conclusion about the effectiveness of self-regulation by professional associations is negative. No one believes in—or even knows about the existence of—the Medical Council of India which, according to one source, is dominated by elites and is unconcerned about field practitioners. In turn, the Indian Medical Association has been called 'reactive', 'useless', and 'worthless'.

Departmental Dominance

The departmental environment of the committees has considerable bearing on the products of committees, especially in the case of 'conflict-resolution' committees. Opinions about departmental influence varied, but most respondents agreed that the departments try to influence the direction of the debates. Our study indicates that departmental influence is strong from the beginning until the end of the committee process in both countries:

- The department initiates the establishment of a committee.
- The department determines the mandate/terms of reference of the committee.
- The department provides suggestions about the selection of committee members.
- The department produces the data on which the committee members base their judgements.
- The department takes care of procedural arrangements that influence the course of the debate.
- The departmental observers steer the debate.
- The departmental secretariat writes the interim and final reports.
- A departmental working group takes care of (studies on) the implementation of the committee proposals.

This strong departmental involvement certainly shapes the influence and importance of committee recommendations and the factors (technocratic and otherwise) on which these are based.

Respondents asserted that departmental influence does not always stem from all the eight points mentioned above. Some committees collect their own data, some write their own reports, and some determine their own procedures. In general, however, a department is involved in most of the activities mentioned above, and has an interest in influencing the outcome of committee deliberations. The committee, on the other hand, also has an interest in keeping up to date on departmental wishes in general, and the (deputy) minister's agenda in particular. Contacts with the department are necessary in order to investigate the expected fate of possible recommendations. Committees that do not keep in touch with political reality produce recommendations that are useless.

Analysis of committee/department interaction needs to recognize that departments are not monoliths. Different sections or bureaus have different interests. In education, for example, whereas the Financial Economic Directorate of a department tends to identify with the finance ministry and its rules, the Primary Education Directorate identifies more with the provider and consumer organizations. Within these directorates, different ideologies struggle for dominance.

In the case of the pupil-bound budget, the Primary Education Directorate was divided into factions. The personal interest of the deputy minister had given the consumer-oriented faction the upper hand but, after the elections, it was uncertain whether she would return so the producer-oriented faction started to organize. During periods of cabinet formation, departments have to keep the engine running (as it were) but are not allowed to make major decisions. The 1998 formation-period took exceptionally long, which delayed all departmental plans, including that for the introduction of the pupil-bound budget. During this period without political leadership, the producer-oriented faction within the ministry took power, and the new deputy minister—who was not an educationalist, and was more managerial than substance-oriented—adopted their ideas. As a consequence, the committee proposals no longer have much departmental support.

The Rispens Committee exemplifies the importance of elections, good timing, and the length of governing periods. Equally important are personal contacts with influential bureaucrats. The transfer of one bureaucrat can change the prospects of a complete policy line. Likewise, professional advisors are an important source of departmental influence in a committee. The position of the professional observers, however, is awkward. While obliged to steer the committee, they are officially not permitted to act unless requested by the committee. They depend on the influence of the Member-Secretary; hence departments that decide to contract an external observer lose an important source of influence. The outsider may well balance between the department and the committee, but is unlikely to be as loyal as a departmental employee.

The absence in committee reports of substantial sections on implementation fits the Dutch tradition of consensus-seeking. It is perceived to be wiser to agree first on the general idea 'in principle', and then discuss the details with the stakeholders in the implementation phase. This procedure takes a lot of time but, on the other hand, prevents the department from making big mistakes.

Research on the Dutch committees revealed that these are under substantial departmental influence. The Indian interviews provide a similar picture. Very much like in the Netherlands, Indian bureaucrats and politicians take no chances in the selection phase. One respondent asserts that 99 per cent of bureaucrats and politicians never invite experts unless they already agree with their viewpoints, and hence, it is no surprise that officers of professional bodies follow ministers like a 'court entourage'. As in the Netherlands, departments influence committees through member-secretaries or (unlike in the Netherlands) through direct instructions by a high official. Expert advice that differs from what was wanted is often wasted, as in the Netherlands. The role of the expert is to avoid the making of capital mistakes, not to formulate the most promising policy option. This observation dovetails with the majority opinion about the (lack of) use of data. Committees are not intended to gather facts, but to serve the purpose of legitimization. Many professionals do not bother about content, but suffer from what someone called 'committee-itis', that is the desire to belong to as many committees as possible.

The information about the permanent advisory bodies in the education sector—the National Institute of Educational Planning and Administration (NIEPA) and the National Council of Educational Research and Training (NCERT)—is not straightforward. Most respondents regard them as repositories of special knowledge set up for the explicit purpose of providing policy advice. According to several respondents, however, NCERT and NIEPA have lately become state directed, or 'subordinated to the ministry'. Another claimed that when Indira Gandhi had a strong desire to implement several plans, NIEPA and NCERT were asked to prepare a technical paper in order to justify this policy. And a third respondent sketched an even more critical view of NIEPA by stating that it played a significant role in the countrywide review of the 1980s that generated dissatisfaction with the existing policy. Discussions were held but, in the end, bureaucrats applied their diversionary tactics and nothing happened. The majority of respondents, however, regarded the twin institutes as closely related to the education department, and as powerless bodies lacking any real authority of their own.

It is widely agreed that technical expertize in both the education and health departments in India is weak and gradually declining. Many respondents observe an erosion of professional and technical control because generalist officers of the Indian Administrative Service (IAS) are moving in everywhere. This trend may be enforced by the fact that appointments are increasingly political instead of merit-based. According to one respondent, the decrease of professional educational knowledge among bureaucrats and politicians has reinforced the professionalization of education itself.

On the other hand, he argued that despite the decline in substance-skills, 'the government still controls and directs all physical and monetary resources'.

One would expect that the decline of professional knowledge in departments would increase their dependency on professional associations, and some respondents argued that the role and policy influence of professionals and experts (particularly of the two professional teacher associations) has indeed increased since 1986. Bureaucrats cannot as easily make decisions without referring to data, so they increasingly depend on national institutes like NIEPA and NCERT. In addition, there often also is a panel of academics and intellectual advisors in which the minister or high bureaucrat has confidence. On the other hand, our respondents also noted that bureaucrats and politicians use data only for legitimization purposes, if at all. If that is true, the influence of the professional institutes must not be overestimated. 'The problem of the professional bureaucrats is that the bureaucrats run the show in this country. Technocrats don't have decision-making power. They tend to be submissive.'

The relatively independent private sector might have a higher degree of technocratic influence. According to one source, however, the private sector does not belong to doctors and physicians anymore but to petty traders and businessmen. It has been thoroughly commercialized. Another respondent expects that the expansion of information technology might divert control to either professionals or business (whichever masters the new skills) but the bureaucrats will lag behind. Finally, the political decision-making that prevails in temporary advisory committees does not create a favourable setting for technocratic influence.

As a last point, it was often noted that within the Indian bureaucracy there is an 'unhealthy competition among ministries over getting foreign money'. Many respondents suggested that health and education rarely win this competition because these fields have low status and because the social ministries in India are typically weak ministries. When the 1983 National Health Policy was approved by the Lok Sabha, fewer than 50 persons, and only 17 MPs, were in the chamber, which indicates the low priority of the field. The same observer explained the lack of interest by the fact that, when ill, the socio-political elites seek sophisticated and complicated health care abroad so the real elite leaders are not personally involved in domestic Indian health policy. Others, however, explained the failure of medical self-regulating systems by elite dominance of the regulatory bodies. Present or not, the elites fail to have a positive impact on health policy.

Committee Influence

Government support is important for the fate of committee recommendations. Recommendations that lack government support have no future. The fact that most plans did (and do) receive government support stems from the fact that most committees produce reports that are in line with government plans. This pattern suggests that committees are merely hired guns in the hands of bureaucrats and politicians, and some of our findings support this suggestion:

- Most committee reports contain only a negligible section on practical steps for implementation. Because departmental work groups develop scenarios for implementation on the basis of committee recommendations, a department has the opportunity to modify proposals according to its preferences. Several respondents were frustrated by the transformations (or, according to some, 'mutilations') of the formally adopted recommendations into politically feasible plans in the implementation phase.
- Committee members are rarely requested to participate in follow-up procedures. Even when an identifiable individual was responsible for drafting (most of) the implementation section, and would have been a logical choice, the department appeared to prefer to handle this phase without outsider interference.
- Committee hearings with stakeholders, at which (deputy) ministers often speak, serve more to convince the stakeholders of departmental plans than to exchange ideas and information.
- The departmental influence at all stages as described in the previous section.
- Known adversaries of intended government policies are not invited to join a temporary advisory committee or blue-ribbon commission.

Despite these findings, the Dutch respondents did not endorse the conjecture that temporary advisory committees are automatically tools in the hands of government. It was noted that several committees refused to follow the government line. The Biesheuvel Committee refused to provide the quick sub-advice sought by Simons and thus prolonged the deputy minister's struggle with medical specialists. The Bruins-Slot Committee went as far as to embarrass its founder by the formulation of propositions that ran contrary to the department's intentions and were no less than a disqualification of the very basics of Simon's Health Care Policy. The De Jager Committee formulated proposals that were overly progressive at that time, and so had no chance to obtain political approval.

However, government has three stock responses to deal with such mutinous committees:

- The establishment of follow-up committees, usually with a chair known to be an adversary of the original committee's recommendations, and with a mandate sufficiently vague to ensure unworkable outcomes.
- The establishment of departmental 'work-groups' which translate the recommendations into practices for implementation that do not challenge the government's position.
- Delayed presentation of committee reports.

One can conclude that governmental and departmental influence on the committees is substantial, but it would be unwise to suggest that committees serve only as hired guns. Despite political and bureaucratic pressure, committees occasionally resist such pressure and come up with unexpected recommendations. On the other hand, of course, a major deviation from the government line seriously reduces the chance for a quick and effective implementation of committee recommendations.

While the influence of most Dutch committees may have been substantial (whether directly tangible or on a more abstract 'meta-level'), it has not been revolutionary. Even the Dekker report, which has a reputation of being revolutionary, merely repackaged sentiments and organizational ideas that had already permeated politics, the government apparatus, and society as a whole. Committees appear unable to change the organizational landscape, but they have been useful instruments to speed up developments that were already planned, to influence social and political debates, and to put issues on the political agenda. The fact that reports that deal with sensitive matters are never delivered shortly before elections and that presentations are usually delayed until after scheduled elections, indicates that politicians do take at least the political consequences of the reports very seriously.

The suggestion that committees are only influential as long as their recommendations are in line with the already existing government plans is not supported by committee members. Despite their voiced frustration about time-delays and alterations in the implementation phase, respondents are generally satisfied about the role and influence of their respective committee. Yet the same respondents suggest that temporary committees have limited influence. Clearly an inconsistency exists which may be explained by the Dutch tendency neither to promise too much nor to expect too little.

To conclude, preliminary analyses suggest that the influence of Dutch temporary advisory committees is limited, but not inconsequential. In both education and health care sectors, many recommendations have been followed, albeit partially altered. Interviews with members of the Dekker Committee, for example, indicate that although the intended wholesale reform plan was discarded, many parts of the plan have been implemented (see also Okma 1997). A similar pattern emerges from the Dunning Committee (van der Grinten 1997). Likewise, committees have generated unintended effects due to anticipatory behaviour by stakeholders. Agents act long before the recommendations are completed and do not wait for the results that they fear. As a consequence, while committee plans may not be adopted in their entirety as government policy, they may already have become partially realized in practice.

However, the complete independence of committees is questionable. In practice, if committees want to have an effect, they cannot afford to neglect departmental intentions and orientations. Committees therefore move strategically back and forth between their own preferences and those of the relevant department. While not necessarily bad or inappropriate, this pattern must be acknowledged. Likewise, the implementation phase that follows the recommendations of a committee often takes so long that the implementation itself produces new problems. The pace of the follow-up phase decreases the relevance as well as the influence of advisory committees. In sum, committees are unable to change the political landscape, but they have been useful instruments to speed up developments that were already planned, to influence social and political debates, and to put issues on the political agenda. The processes of anticipatory behaviour further add to committee influence.

The influence of the Central government in policy-making is strong even when education and health are state subjects. One Indian respondent noted that policy inputs come entirely from the Centre which then enforces its recommendations through what he called 'the power of the exchequer'. For example, when the Centre raised the salaries of academic staff in institutions of higher learning, the states could do the same for their own institutions because the Central government promised to reimburse 80 per cent of the cost. The current District Primary Education Programme is being funded with Central funds. Other respondents argued that in the field of health, states do not have a policy worth the name. States only pursue money from whatever source may be available. States implement such programmes that are funded by the Government of India or international donor agencies and follow the guidelines set by them, but they do not continue these programmes with state-raised resources after the initial stimulus programme has ended.

Follow-up Steps

Quite often, Dutch committee members discuss and defend their proposals throughout the country (Welschen, Rispens, Biesheuvel, Dunning). With the notable exceptions of Rispens, van Eijndhoven, and Biesheuvel Committee reports rarely contain a section on implementation. Departmental work groups (sometimes together with experts from the field) usually develop implementation plans on the basis of the committee recommendations, but committee members are rarely involved in this follow-up procedure. Two reports lead to the establishment of new committees, and two committee members (from different committees) were requested to conduct follow-up studies.

The Indian interviews suggest that all good intentions and sensible plans are eventually killed in the implementation phase. One respondent bluntly stated that there is no implementation because many policies are not even supposed to be implemented; he said that government initiates policies that it knows won't take off because '. . . then you would at least be doing something'. Respondents regularly characterized Indian policies as diversionary tactics. A general theme was that because governments cannot admit that current laws are not implementable, they announce the prospects of a new policy. Such announcements buy time and enable the policy-maker to put critics into committee and advisory bodies where they can be contained. Another respondent argued that the establishment of a political committee serves no other goal than the obstruction of an unwelcome policy from a previous era.

Once formulated, the main purpose of policy documents appears to be as a source of quotes. To cite two representative views, 'The 1983 National Health Policy has little impact/relevance other than being quoted from time to time' and 'the *Challenge of Education* document was not implemented and now is so old that it should be consigned to a waste-basket. Instead it is still being quoted.' One respondent observed that the latter document contained no financial paragraph on purpose because such a paragraph would highlight the lack of a sound financial basis for the implementation of the many plans listed in the report. Financial implications of a policy are rarely worked out because they would just 'complicate' matters. As a consequence, many unrealistic plans are drafted that are destined to gather dust in a cupboard or at best be quoted occasionally.

It should be noted that Dutch committee reports also often lack a substantial implementation chapter, perhaps for comparable reasons. The Dutch ministries do not wish to attract opposition and therefore postpone the writing of sections on 'next steps' for implementation. The difference between the two countries is that in the Netherlands, the implementation chapter is marginalized because a department wishes to increase the prospects for implementation, whereas (according to many Indian respondents) implementation in India is never a goal. 'Policy-making in India is an exercise in setting goals, not in translating them into reality.'

As an evident example, the highest committee on health affairs in India appears to be designed for ineffectiveness. The Central Committee on Health is composed of all state-level health ministers plus the corresponding health secretaries in the relevant departments. Logistically it is enormously difficult to convene all these agents and, when convened, to provide an actionable agenda. Every state has its say, and reports of the standing committee consist of compromises that nobody opposes but that nobody favours cither. Worse yet, the committee never takes the plans of the National Economic Development Council or the Planning Commission into consideration, so nothing is ever translated into practice. Since the national bureaucracy also consults all the states before enacting anything, the process is guaranteed to grind to a halt.

However, the CABE is constituted in a similar way, with all state-level education ministers plus the corresponding education secretaries in relevant departments. Yet, CABE has played an important role in planning more practical aspects of educational policy and in getting them approved by the states. For example, a recommendation from the Board about the decentralization of educational management has now been accepted as part of the national policy. Nonetheless, changes are markedly slow and difficult to achieve.

One Indian respondent noted that in 1985 it was decided not to establish yet another standing committee because there were already too many reports, none of which had been implemented. This observation parallels the Dutch *Raad op Maat* policy that took the attitude one step further and actually abolished the majority of the existing advisory bodies.

Chapter 7

Professionals and Public Policy: The Technocratic Hypothesis Revisited

OUR IDPAD PROJECT was triggered by curiosity about the rising influence of technocracy in public policy-making. In both countries of our study, the Netherlands and India, this trend toward technocratization has been stimulated by recent thrusts towards modernization and administrative change. Pursuit of ambitious development programmes served to strengthen the technocratic orientation of public administration. Currently, the Netherlands is enmeshed in changes induced not only by its membership of the European Union but in the overall transition from a welfare state to a neo-liberal state. India's economic environment has also been changing to adapt to the dominant paradigm of neo-liberalism that requires macro-management of the economy.

The rise in the influence of technocrats has evolved gradually in the Netherlands as the middle class has expanded with the rise in education. This process has been of a shorter duration in India. Compared to the total population, professionally trained Indians have remained a small minority, but their influence has grown disproportionately to their size. Initially, the process of planned development and growth in public sector enterprises led to a high demand for scientific and technical professionals. At the cost of basic literacy and primary education, technical education received significant attention and public finance. The consequence was the creation of one of the largest pools of technical personnel in the world. After 1991, when economic reforms were initiated, technocrats have been in demand because of administrative change within and outside government.

As acknowledged in Chapter 1, there are various ways through which experts and technocrats may influence government, and we hence chose to focus attention on the channel of committees that were appointed by the government to provide specific advice. Increasingly, governments were turning away from in-house expertize in favour of external experts, and advisory committees were the vehicles to convene such experts for collective activity. While a considerable amount of literature has analysed the role of bureaucracy and administrative institutions in formulating government policy, there has been little research attention paid on the way the outside experts are mobilized to give advice or on the way this advice is processed for policy formulation. While Wheare (1955) is a classic commentary on the British Constitution and while Plowden (1987) describes the institutional policy advice within various governments, neither contribution examines the dynamics of expert advisory committees and the way their advice is processed.

This study has attempted to fill these lacunae in the studies of public administration and public policy. Our findings are based on extensive interviews of those who were themselves involved in this committee process. Although the evidence about the policy-shaping activities of the advisory committees may be inconclusive, it presents interesting empirical insights on how the policy processes actually work. The study, therefore, concludes by offering some hypothesis for continuing work in the field.

Committees and Technocracy in India

The study began by hypothesizing that technocratization of decision-making correlates significantly with the emergence of a large, important middle class and, by extension, that technocratization deepens or becomes more pervasive with increasing wealth and well-being. Although the evidence about the policy-shaping activities of advisory committees is not conclusive, it may be because middle class interests have enveloped the entire process. It can be argued that technocratic skills become yet another weapon to maintain privilege or even to make it more secure, and such a trend exacerbates inequality.

The basic policy choice is invariably produced by the committee appointed for the purpose. The committee encourages widest public participation and, where necessary, it commissions specialist reports on important areas of policy. Some of the salient features of the government approach appear to be that, even before a committee is set up, the government spends time in formulating suitable terms of reference for it. The terms of reference set the agenda as well as the way the committee is likely to function.

The choice of the chairperson is also critical. Although almost invariably well known to the appointing authority, the person must be generally acceptable to other members of the committee. The reputation and the public standing of the chairman as well as the members of a committee also enhance the likelihood that its recommendations will be accepted.

The appointment of a secretary is critical. To a great extent the secretary determines the kind of background work that needs to be done to provide a basis for discussions. He or she is instrumental in searching for relevant documents and identifying experts or knowledgeable persons who may be invited before the committee for consultation. Often the secretary assigns research tasks to outside individuals or agencies.

The style of policy formulation involves extensive advice and consultation. The outstanding feature of policy-making is characterized by accommodation and settlement, involving political, administrative, and specialist groups. In determining India's 1986 Education Policy, extensive consultations took place as the government sought to reach all levels of expertize and interest through numerous seminars held throughout the country. The purpose was to elicit opinion from as many diverse sources, regions, and people as possible.

Another feature of the use of committees is that the recommendations of an expert committee are processed by a political committee, which is usually an all-party group. The Kothari Commission report was repeatedly discussed and refined so that many significant technical suggestions got diluted while those that had political overtones tended to get highlighted. The 1986 policy was also extensively discussed in the Indian parliament but it appears to have been steered well by the then education minister. The Central Advisory Board of Education (CABE), which consisted of state education ministers, also was involved in approving the policy when others sought to revise it in 1992.

The political situation seems to have a strong influence on the way a policy is determined and then implemented. By the time the Kothari Commission produced its recommendations, the government that had appointed it had been replaced. Indira Gandhi was opposed from within her own party, and education was low on her list of priorities. The education minister who had appointed the commission had resigned and someone else had taken over. The latter was enthusiastic but carried little political weight. The result was that even though the Kothari Commission's recommendation influenced thinking, policy changes were slow to occur.

The 1986 policy was formulated with the active involvement of the then Prime Minister, Rajiv Gandhi. Narasimha Rao as education minister played an important role. But implementation of the policy slowed when Rajiv Gandhi lost much of his lustre after 1987 and then lost the elections in 1989. The new government led by V.P. Singh set up another committee to review the 1986 policy. A review report was published but, before it could be taken up, the Singh government had fallen and P.V. Narasimha Rao came in as the new prime minister. The 1986 policy came back with enthusiasm.

By its very nature the policy process is built on compromises. As the membership of committees becomes more and more diverse, the search is not for 'best' solutions but for acceptable ones that may be a considerable dilution of the optimal solutions. In order to stretch its probability of acceptance, a policy may have to make compromises in terms of its thrusts and its technical components. The content of policy will have to be consistent with the level of understanding that the concerned members may have of the technical components. The committees do not provide reasons why some alternatives are accepted and not others.

Indian perceptions about the role of the state are generally negative. Some respondents say that the state is unwilling to do anything because 'politicians have vested interests in illiteracy!' They 'keep the people backwards so it's easier to deal with them'. Most respondents regard the state as incapable of pushing the borders of development. The bureaucracy is generally believed to be the most powerful actor and, consequently, the major obstacle to change. Politicians were rarely mentioned although it was occasionally noted that those who have a strong interest in a subject do set things in motion. Some substantial changes have been formulated by politicians, but the implementation phase usually take long enough for the politicians to disappear and for the bureaucrats to stop the changes. One relatively sanguine respondent remarked on the emergence of new ideas that 'these must be from the bureaucracy. A percolation from academic papers through journalism into the bureaucracy and finally as policy options to the politicians.' This remark is more optimistic about the Indian bureaucracy than the general idea that bureaucracy cannot effect changes, only obstruct them.

Given India's federal system, inter-governmental relations play an important role in service delivery. In both health and education, resources and policy inputs come from the Centre while implementation is at the state level. But in neither policy field does this division of tasks work effectively. 'National health policy doesn't make much of a difference, because it's the state governments that have to implement it . . . and they don't', said one respondent. Another claimed 'there is no health policy worth the name at the state level' while a third noted that 'education policy formulation take place at the state level, but the states are absorbed by day-to-day problems and do nothing'.

Mistrust of the possibilities of the state is widely shared. Many states see the Central government only as a revenue stream. Even if the Centre's schemes or projects do not fit into a state's own priorities, the latter takes the money because—as one respondent commented—money is what makes Central decisions so important. Another respondent asserted that the states are not completely to blame for their bad performance record because the Centre neglects to consider the capacities and resources of the states in the implementation phase, and consequently formulates policies that are highly unrealistic. The biggest mistake policy-makers make is to think that policy formulation equals policy implementation. According to some cynics, this is not an issue of misconception but a fact of interest representation: 'it is in the interest of the Centre to have a weak state and vice versa, so that one can blame the other'.

The low amount of trust in the state is equalled by the high amount of faith in the possibilities for development and change at the district level. However, the respondents do not indicate the basis for this optimism in the lower ranks. In view of the elsewhere mentioned obstruction to local initiatives taken by state bureaucrats, politicians, and local health/education providers, this optimism is surprising. One respondent did note that local small-scale initiatives get marginalized quickly without help from the Centre. There is no reason to assume that this pattern of behaviour would not hold for the district level, too.

The solution for the problematic division of tasks between states and the Centre in India has been sought in efforts toward decentralization. These efforts have been blocked by bureaucrats who do not want to lose their power to agents at the district or lower levels. According to one outspoken respondent, the states routinely say that they want decentralization in order to escape Central interference, but the state-level politicians and bureaucrats do not want to share power. Therefore, lower level institutions such as the Panchayati Raj institutions are not funded, and the total framework does not work. This is a dilemma because service delivery systems for health and education cannot be isolated nor operate in a vacuum; local level participation is essential for such labour-intensive services.

Ironically, the providers are often not very favourably inclined toward decentralization efforts either. According to one very senior and experienced respondent, school teachers do not want supervision and therefore oppose Panchayati Raj. Another respondent described how attempts to provide health care through the Community Development Programme were frustrated by lack of co-operation from local physicians. They were simply not interested and vitiated the local health programme. In one sense, government reciprocates by not facilitating private initiative. Several respondents noted that many bureaucratic roadblocks were encountered when trying to obtain permits and one even claimed that government deliberately destabilizes anyone who begins to achieve something. Another said that the emergence of an enabling government is not to be expected soon: 'Elsewhere there has been a change from a pre-emptive style of government to an enabling style but not in India; everyone here wants to rule rather than to run things effectively.'

Nonetheless, there are some signs of liberalization even in the sector for delivering health services. In Rajasthan, the introduction of an alternative way of funding allows hospitals to keep their own funds (raised through fees) rather than handing them back to the state treasury as long as this money is re-invested in the hospital itself. Through government sanctioned 'welfare societies' for self-regulation and public audit, hospitals (over 100 beds) are allowed to charge fees for services as well as for certain supplies. Another recent change in health policy throughout India has been to welcome direct foreign investment by non-resident Indians (NRI) who are willing to set up local institutions in India in anticipation of the day when they themselves return from overseas.

The importance of the private sector in health care is recognized by most respondents—some only grudgingly, others more enthusiastically. One observed that 'concepts of corporatism are penetrating the whole health sector' while another suggested that the private sector at district level is not only surviving but multiplying because the people regard it as better than government-provided care. Yet many other respondents cautioned that the private health sector no longer belongs to physicians or doctors but rather to petty traders and businessmen interested only in profit. They also pointed to the lack of regulatory mechanisms for supervising and disciplining medical providers, whether private or public, including the self-regulatory arrangements allegedly characteristic of professionals. The private provision of health care services is a subject that merits systematic examination and research in India—particularly given its almost total neglect during the past half century (Berman 1998).

Indian policy-making seems to be dominated by bureaucrats. These bureaucrats who are recruited in a centralized fashion and are transferred from field jobs as heads of districts to positions in the state governments serve in the federal government which has more advisory and regulatory functions in the fields of education and health. Ministers are not recruited on the basis on expertize. They represent constituencies and come into the cabinet because of their organizational or political skills. A few ministries like those of finance or law have usually had ministers with relevant training or experience. Whenever individuals with some professional expertize have become members of cabinets, the prime minister has not utilized their expertize by allotting the concerned portfolios (Mathur and Björkman 1994). The result is that the government works on the basis of large networks of committees that are both formal and informal. Indian policy-makers tend to appoint committees for all the reasons that Dutch policy-makers do, but they do so also in order to seek genuine policy advice when they find that bureaucratic advice alone will not do.

Dominance and Atmosphere in the Netherlands

To parody Aldous Huxley, all committee members are influential but some exercise more influence than others. Professional expertize, high energy levels, public prestige, and being the chairperson were mentioned as causes for individual dominance. Dominant chairmen included de Jager, Stekelenburg, Biesheuvel (only on matters of procedure), Dunning, and Dekker—until the latter fell ill and Dunning became the most influential member of that committee. Van Eijndhoven, Rispens, Dekker and Welschen all had committee members who dominated because of a combination of their capacities and the amount of work they put into the committee. The three members of the Bruins-Slot Committee appear to have worked on equal footing, except for the departmental 'spy' who was not trusted and therefore kept out of some important meetings and activities.

The commitment of an influential politician or bureaucrat can provide a way out of the common situation of deadlock in a committee. Many respondents mentioned particular bureaucrats and/or politicians who 'got things moving'. Unfortunately, such dependence on individual initiatives brings no continuity at all. Because of the unstable political situation, careers are often short-lived, and the defendants of the *status quo* can successfully perform their delaying tactics. The eventual influence of charismatic and entrepreneurial leaders is therefore often disappointing.

Most committees appear to have operated in relative harmony although Bruins-Slot, Welschen and Biesheuvel were said to experience a considerable degree of conflict. It has to be noted, however, that different members of the same committee did not always agree on the atmosphere. In fact, sometimes respondents from within the same committee provided different stories about the same event, which methodologically suggests the continuing validity of the Roshomon Principle in social enquiry. To provide the flavour without over-exaggerating the effect, several cases are provided below.

In the Welschen Committee, for example, one respondent said that the political battle between the departments was fought by the professional advisors only, not within the committee; another, however, claimed that Welschen was a battle from start to finish. In the Biesheuvel Committee, one respondent said that the committee operated smoothly; another argued that the amateur status of many committee members in the field of health care caused a great deal of (admittedly creative) conflict and chaos. According to several members of the Dunning Committee, the chair kept the departmental advisors out of the debate, while a third member asserted that they seriously influenced the committee. One respondent also said that party politics did not interfere with Dunning Committee's operation, while another felt that at least one committee member presented himself as a party representative. As for the Dekker Committee, one respondent felt that Dekker's preference for the 'market' principle emerged along the way, while his committee colleague argued that Dekker was very assertive as chair and that he had pushed the market principle fiercely from the beginning. While none of these examples is overwhelmingly important, they do underscore the 'degrees of freedom' involved in exploratory research through interviews, howsoever modestly structured.

Present Dutch policy-making is thoroughly technocratic. Experts are recruited into highly specialized civil service departments. Experts are recruited as ministers. Specialization is increasingly evident in parliament due to its committee system based on policy sectors. Experts are found as Crown members of the SER, in numerous advisory councils and royal commissions, and in the many forecasting and fact-finding agencies that surround government. Experts can also be found within the organizations that challenge government's power and try to influence policy formation by providing parliament with facts and data. Finally, experts are found in the temporary advisory committees that are appointed to buy time when controversial issues arise. Dutch policy-makers regularly resort to the establishment of temporary advisory committees with a technical nature as a means of depoliticizing debates and thus maintaining social harmony.

The influence of the committee reports varies considerably. It has to be noted that not all mandates were equally ambitious, and that comparisons are potentially deceitful. However, some broad conclusions can be drawn. First, most respondents made a distinction between the direct, tangible effects of a committee and the more abstract 'meta' influence of the report. Influential committees in the direct sense were Biesheuvel, van Eijndhoven, and Rispens. Committees that influenced the social and political debate, and influenced other committees, were those of Dekker and Dunning and (on a different scale) Welschen and Biesheuvel. Members of the Willems Committee also mentioned that their recommendations were one of the main reasons for the withdrawal of the Dekker master plan.

Second, several Dutch respondents expressed disappointment with the implementation phase in which formally adopted committee recommendations are transformed by operational departments into allegedly feasible plans. In order to ensure compliance with original intentions, they argued that committee recommendations should be explicit and unambiguous. Reports that contain compromises leave room for multiple interpretations which are useless or even counterproductive. Most respondents were unhappy about the delay that accompanies the implementation of recommendations. Some asserted that politicians and bureaucrats should stop negotiating and simply push their plans through. On the other hand, one respondent claimed that the biggest mistake of the Dunning Committee was not to involve the stakeholders and interest groups in the development of recommendations, which put the report in isolation.

Propositions for Further Investigation

Despite initial skepticism about whether comparisons between the Netherlands and India would yield fruitful results, there are similarities and mutual lessons to be learned about the ways in which policy processes work through advisory committees and commissions. As research projects often generate as many questions as they do answers, the following non-prioritized list provides propositions or empirically grounded hypotheses for future investigation:

1. The higher the consensus in society on an issue, the more 'bottom-up' policy-making can work because differences are marginal/incremental; the lower the consensus, the more is 'top-down' policy-making required although implementation becomes less probable.
2. Expert advisory committees tend to neutralize problems and clarify facts; they professionalize the solutions as well as legitimize, and sometimes publicize, them.
3. Comparisons between the two human capital policy sectors reveal that education is more politicized whereas health is perceived to be more technical or have technocratic solutions and hence is de-politicized.
4. Dynamics within advisory committees in India and the Netherlands are relatively similar, but their terms of reference differ: Dutch committees are relatively narrowly focused on specific problems of implementation, while Indian committees are very widely geared toward direction-setting.

5. Timeframes have an impact on findings, hence, historical sequencing becomes important. Today Dutch society is largely consensual on basic values while Indian society remains pluralistic and heterodox. Feasible policies for human capital require implementation over periods of decades and centuries rather than only months and years.
6. The operational/behavioural boundaries between categories of policy actors—politicians, experts, bureaucrats—are often blurred and fuzzy; one specific actor may play different roles at different times, or even at the same time.

These propositions not only provide an ever opening array of avenues for research, but also summarize practical relevance for policy applications. An important focus of public policy studies is their ability to investigate the actual ways in which government institutions work in order to formulate public policy and then implement it. An early example was *The Essence of Decision* (Allison 1971) which was concerned with how the US Presidency processed information throughout the Cuban missile crisis of 1960.

Such detailed and introspective investigations are, of course, difficult to make unless the participants themselves are willing to unravel and explain the processes and to allow an outside view of their internal procedures. In general, government has been slow to recognize and respond to the rise of technocratic influence in policy. Hopefully, this study has provided some preliminary insights into this complex process.

Appendix 1
Lists of Advisory Committees

Membership of Indian Committees

HEALTH SURVEY AND DEVELOPMENT COMMITTEE (BHORE COMMITTEE), 1943

Sir Joseph Bhore (Chairman)

Dr R.A. Amesur
President, Indian Medical Association

Rai Bahadur Dr A.C. Bannerjea
Director of Public Health, United Provinces

Khan Bahadur Dr A.H. Butt
Director of Public Health, Punjab

Dr R.B. Chandrachud
Chief Medical Officer, Baroda State

Colonel E. Cotter
Public Health Commissioner, Government of India

Dr D.J.R. Dadabhoy
Ex-President, All India Association of Medical Women, Bombay

Dr J.B. Grant
Director, All-India Institute of Hygiene and Public Health, Calcutta

Khan Bahadur Dr A.M. Hameed
Member, Medical Council of India; Professor of Pathology, Lucknow University

Lt General Sir Bennet Hance
Director General, Indian Medical Service

Sir Henry Holland
C.M.S. Hospital, Quetta

Sir Fredrick James
Member, Central Advisory Board of Health

N.M. Joshi (MLA)

Lt Colonel H.M. Lazarus
Chief Medical Officer, Women's Medical Service

Pandit L.K. Maitra (MLA)
Member, Central Advisory Board of Health

Diwan Bahadur Dr Sir Lakshnaswami Mudaliar
Vice Chancellor, Madras University

Dr U.B. Narayanrao
President, All-India Medical Licentiates Association

Dr Vishwa Nath
Member, Medical Council of India

Major-General W.C. Paton
Surgeon General, Government of Bengal

Dr B.C. Roy
President, Medical Council of India

The Honourable P.N. Sapru
Member, Council of State; Member, Central Advisory Board of Health

Lt Colonel B.Z. Shah
Superintendent, Mental Hospital, Poona

B. Shiva Rao
Mrs K. Shaffi Tyabji

Dr H.R. Wadhwani
Minister of Public Health, Sind

Rao Bahadur Dr K.C.K.E. Raja (Secretary)

Joint Secretaries

Dr M. Ahmed

Captain A. Bannerji

Dr K.T. Jungalwala

Rai Bahadur Man Mohan

Rao Bahadur Dr S. Ramakrishnan

COMMITTEE ON INDIGENOUS SYSTEMS OF MEDICINE
(CHOPRA COMMITTEE), 1948

Colonel Sir R.N. Chopra (Chairman)

Vaids (*practitioners of Ayurvedic medicine*)

Bishagratna Dr A. Lakshmipathi
Principal, Madras Ayurvedic College; Member, Board of Advisers on Indigenous Systems of Medicine, Madras

Dr Balakrishna Chintamani Lagu (MLA)
President, Board of Indian Systems of Medicine, Bombay

Dr B.A. Pathak
Principal, Benaras Hindu University Ayurvedic College; Member, UP Board of Indian Medicine

Hakims (practitioners of Unani medicine)

Shifa-ul-Mulk Hakim Habib-ur-Rehaman
Principal Tibbia College, Dacca

Hakim Naseer-ud-din Ahmed Khan
General Secretary of the Ayurvedic and Tibbi Board, Delhi Province

Allopaths (practitioners of Western medicine)

Major M.H. Shah
Superintendent, Irwin Hospital, Delhi (subsequently Lt Colonel and Chief Medical Officer, Jinnah Central Hospital, Karachi)

Dr B.N. Ghosh
Professor of Pharmacology, Carmichael Medical College, Calcutta

Given representations by the Health Department that there were no representatives of the orthodox Vaidyas on the Committee, Vaidya Jadavjee Tricumjee and Dr A.U. Bhatt (Principal, Tibbia College, Aligarh) were appointed.

HEALTH SURVEY AND PLANNING COMMITTEE
(MUDALIAR COMMITTEE), 1959

Dr Lakshmanaswami Mudaliar (Chairman)
Vice-Chancellor, Madras University

Shri Tirumal Rao (MP)

Dr G.S. Melkote (MP)

Lt Colonel V. Srinivasan
Director General of Health Services, Ministry of Health, New Delhi

Lt General D.N. Chakravarti
Director, Health Services; Secretary, Health Department, Government of West Bengal, Calcutta

Major K.N. Rao
Director of Medical Services, Hyderabad

Dr K.C.E. Raja
Vice Chancellor, Kerala University, Trivandrum

Dr Dukhan Ram
Ex-Vice Chancellor, Bihar University, Patna

Dr C.G. Pandit
Director, Indian Council of Medical Research, New Delhi

Dr H.M. Lazarus
Professor of Obstetrics and Gynaecology, KG Medical College, Vishakhapatnam

Dr C.O. Karunakaran
Ex-President, India Medical Association, Trivandrum

Lt General B. Chaudhri (retd)
Director General, Armed Forces Medical Service

Lt General B.M. Rao (retd)
Director General, Armed Forces Medical Service

Dr R.V. Sathe, Bombay

Dr P. Mehta
Ex-Director, Jamnagar Research Institute, Jamnagar

Dr T.R. Tewari
Director, Central Health Service, New Delhi (Secretary)

COMMITTEE ON MULTI-PURPOSE WORKERS UNDER HEALTH AND FAMILY PLANNING PROGRAMME (KARTAR SINGH COMMITTEE), 1972-3

Kartar Singh (Chairman)
Additional Secretary, Ministry of Health and Family Planning, Government of India

Dr J.B. Srivastava
Director General of Health Services, Government of India (Vice-Chairman)

K.N. Srivastava
Commissioner Health and Family Planning, Government of Uttar Pradesh

S.E. Sukhthankar
Secretary, Health Department, Government of Maharashtra

H.M. Singh
Secretary, Department of Health and Family Planning, Government of Tamil Nadu

Dr P.R. Sondhi
Director of Health Services, Government of Haryana

Dr V.H. Thakore
Director of Health Services, Government of Gujarat

Dr A. Timmapaya
Director, National Institute Health Administration and Education, New Delhi

A. Prasad
Deputy Secretary, Planning Commission, Government of India

Dr P. Dinesh
Commissioner, Rural Health and Mobile Hospitals, Government of India

Dr D.N. Gupta
Deputy Commissioner, Department of Family Planning, Ministry of Health and Family Planning, Government of India (Member-Secretary)

COMMITTEE ON MEDICAL EDUCATION AND SUPPORT MANPOWER (SRIVASTAVA COMMITTEE), 1974

Dr J.B. Srivastava (Chairman)
Director General of Health Services

Dr C. Gopalan, Director General, Indian Council of Medical Research, New Delhi

Professor V. Ramalingaswami
Director, All-India Institute of Medical Sciences, New Delhi

Dr P.N. Chuttani
Director, Post-Graduate Institute of Medical Education and Research, Chandigarh

Shri J.P. Naik
Member-Secretary, Indian Council of Social Science Research, New Delhi

Shri C.R. Krishnamurti
Director, Ministry of Health and Family Planning

Dr Sharad Kumar
Deputy Director General of Health Services (Medical) (Member-Secretary)

COMMITTEE ON 'HEALTH FOR ALL: AN ALTERNATIVE STRATEGY' (ICMR–ICSSR COMMITTEE), 1981

V. Ramalingaswami (Chairman)

R.S. Arole

B.J. Coyaji

N.S. Deodhar

N. Jungalwalla

C.R. Krishnamurti

J.P. Naik

V.N. Rao

S. Sankaran

Narottam Shah

B.N. Sinha

V Subhadra

K.N. Udupa

N.H. Antia (member-secretary)

EXPERT REVIEW COMMITTEE FOR HEALTH MANPOWER PLANNING AND DEVELOPMENT (BAJAJ COMMITTEE), 1986

Professor J.S. Bajaj (Chairman)
Professor of Medicine, All India Institute of Medical Sciences, New Delhi

Dr Harcharan Singh
Joint Adviser (Health), Planning Commission

Shri Satya Bhushan
Director, National Institute of Education Planning and Administration, New Delhi

Shri A.M. Nimbalkar
Director General of Employment and Training/Joint Secretary, Ministry of Labour (or his nominee)

Dr J.P. Gupta
Joint Director, National Institute of Health and Family Welfare

Mrs P.K. Karthiyani
Kaveri Apartments, Alaknanda, New Delhi

Shri S.K. Handa
Deputy Educational Advisor (H), Ministry of Human Resources Development

Dr K.B. Sharma
Deputy Director-General Health Services, New Delhi

COMMISSION ON EDUCATION AND NATIONAL DEVELOPMENT (KOTHARI COMMISSION), 1964-6

Dr D.S. Kothari (Chairman)
Chair, University Grants Commissions; Professor of Physics, University of Delhi

Jean Thomas
Inspector General of Education, France; former Assistant Director-General, UNESCO

Anatoly Shumovsky
Director, Methodological Division, Ministry of Higher and Special Secondary Education, Russian Soviet Federated Socialist Republic; Professor of Physics, Moscow University

Sadatoshi Ihara
Professor, Faculty of Science and Technology, Waseda University, Tokyo

H.L. Evin
Director, Institute of Education, London

Roger Reville
Dean of Research, University of California

A.R. Dawood
Former Director, Extension Programme for Secondary Education, Government of India

R.A. Gopalaswami
Director, Institute of Applied Manpower Research, New Delhi

V.S. Jha
Former Director, Commonwealth Liaison Unit, London

P.N. Kripal
Education Adviser to the Government of India

K.G.M Saiyidain
Former Education Adviser to the Government of India

B.P. Pal
Director, Indian Agricultural Research Institute

M.V. Mathur
Professor of Economics and Public Administration, Rajasthan University, Jaipur

S. Panandiker
Head, Department of Education, Karnataka University

Triguna Sen
Rector, Jadavpur University, West Bengal

J.P. Naik
Head, Department of Education Planning, Administration and Finance, Gokhale Institute of Politics and Economics, Pune, Maharashtra

REVIEW COMMITTEE ON 1986 NATIONAL POLICY ON EDUCATION (RAMAMURTI COMMITTEE), 1990

Acharya Ramamurti (Chairman)
PO Khadigram, District Munger, Bihar

Professor C.N.R. Rao
Director, Indian Institute of Science, Bangalore

Dr Sukhdev Singh
Former Vice-Chancellor, Punjab and MP Agricultural Universities

Dr M. Santappa
Former Vice-Chancellor, Madras University

Dr Obaid Siddiqi
Tata Institute of Fundamental Research, Bombay

Bhaskar Ray Chaudhri
Vice-Chancellor, Calcutta University

Shri MG Bhatwadekar
Former Principal, Maharaja College, Jaipur

Professor Usha Mehta
Political Scientist, University of Bombay

Professor Satchidanand Murty
Sangam Jagarlamudi, Guntur, Andhra Pradesh

Dr Anil Sadgopal
Kishore Bharati, Hoshangabad, Maharashtra

Father T.V. Kunnunkal
Chairman, National Open School, New Delhi

Professor Mrinal Miri
Professor of Philosophy, North-Eastern Hill University, Shillong, Meghalaya

Dr Vidya Niwas Misra
Vice-Chancellor, Kashi Vidyapeeth, Varanasi, Uttar Pradesh

Shri S.Z. Qasim
Vice-Chancellor, Jamia Millia Islamia, New Delhi

Shri Ved Vyas
Chairman, DAV College Management Committee, New Delhi

Shri Manubhai Pancholi
Lok Bharati, Sansora, District Bhavnagar

Shri S. Gopalan
Additional Secretary, Department of Education, Ministry of Human Resource Development, Government of India, New Delhi

CENTRAL ADVISORY BOARD OF EDUCATION
COMMITTEE ON THE RAMAMURTI COMMITTEE REPORT
(JANARDHANA REDDY COMMITTEE), 1991-2

Shri Janardhana Reddy (Chairman)
Chief Minister and Minister of Education, Andhra Pradesh

Shri Vikram Verma
Minister of Education, Madhya Pradesh

Shri Gepong Apang
Chief Minister and Minister of Education, Arunachal Pradesh

Shri R.M. Veerappan
Minister of Education, Tamil Nadu

Dr Ram Chandra Purve
Minister (Secondary Education & Primary Education), Bihar

Shri S.S. Chakraborty
Minister Higher Education, West Bengal

Shri E.T. Mohammed Basheer
Minister of Education, Kerala

Dr Shrimati Chitra Naik
Member (Education), Planning Commission

Professor G. Ram Reddy
Chairman, University Grants Commission

Dr M.S. Adiseshiah
Chairman, Madras Institute of Development Studies, Madras

Dr Radhika Herzberger
Director, Rishi Valley School, Andhra Pradesh

Dr A.P. Mitra
Bhatnagar Fellow, New Delhi

Shri Jagannathan Krishnamal
Secretary, Land for Tillers Freedom, Tanjore, Tamil Nadu

Dr Ram Dayal Munda
Professor of Regional Languages, Ranchi University, Ranchi

Shri Habib Tanvir
Director Naya Theater, New Delhi

Dr R.V. Vaidyanatha Ayyar (Member-Secretary)
Joint Secretary Planning, Department of Education, Ministry of Human Resource Development, Government of India, New Delhi

Permanent invitees to meetings of the Committee:

- Union Education Secretary
- Director, National Council for Educational Research and Training (NCERT)
- Director, National Institute of Education Planning and Administration (NIEPA)

Membership of Dutch Committees

COMMITTEE ON THE STRUCTURE AND FINANCING OF HEALTH CARE (DEKKER COMMITTEE), 1986-7

Dr P.B. Boorsma
Professor in Public Finance, Technical University Twente
Member of Parliament for the Christian Democrats

Dr W. Dekker (Chairman)
Chairman, Supervisory Board, Philips

Dr A.J. Dunning (Deputy-Chairman)
Professor of Cardiology, University of Amsterdam

Dr G.J. Hazenkamp
Director, Foundation of the Nationalist Calvinist Board on Matters of Society, Leuven (Belgium)

Dr H.J.J. Leenen
Professor of Health and Health Care Systems, University of Amsterdam

Mrs J.J.M.S. Leyten-de Wijkerslooth de Weerdesteyn, LLM
Member of the Dutch Senate for the Liberal Conservatives

Dr B.M.S. van Praag
Professor of Mathematical Economy, University of Rotterdam

Two advisers assisted the committee:

- Director-General of Health Care (J. van Londen)
- Director-General of Welfare (A.J. Gijsbers)

COMMITTEE ON CHOICES IN HEALTH CARE (DUNNING COMMITTEE), 1991

Dr A.J. Dunning (Chairman)
Professor of Cardiology, University of Amsterdam

Dr T.E.D. van der Grinten (Deputy-Chairman)
Professor of Management and Organization of Mental Health Care Systems, University of Rotterdam

Dr A. van Dantzig
Psychiatrist, Amsterdam

Dr H.M. Dupuis
Professor of Medical Ethics, University of Leiden

Dr H.A.M.J. ten Have
Professor in Philosophy, Catholic University of Brabant, Nijmegen

Mr H.J. Hubben
Professor of Health Care Law, Catholic University of Brabant, Nijmegen

Mr J.P. Kasdrop (Secretary)
National Health Council, Zoetermeer

Dr B. Meyboom-de Jong
Professor of General Practice Medicine

Dr J.H. Mulder (Deputy-Secretary)
Bureau of Policy Development, Directorate General Health Care, Ministry of Health, Welfare and Sport

Dr D. Post
Professor of Social Medicine, University of Groningen, and Medical Adviser of a Sickness Fund

Dr W.P.M.M. van de Ven
Professor of Insurance for Social Medicine Expenses, University of Rotterdam

The committee was assisted by Dr W. van de Donk (Bureau of the Secretary-General, Ministry of Finance); Dr E.J. Mulock-Houwer (Deputy Director-General of Welfare, Ministry of Health, Welfare and Sport); J. Verhoeff (Director, Psychiatric Care, Ministry of Health, Welfare and Sport); and Dr R.L.J.M. Scheerder (Director of Health Care, Ministry of Health, Welfare and Sport).

COMMITTEE ON MODERNIZING CURATIVE CARE
(BIESHEUVEL COMMITTEE)

Mr B.W. Biesheuvel te Aerdenhout (Chairman)

Dr G.P.L.A. van den Broek
Director, Catherina Hospital, Eindhoven

Dr A.J. Dunning
Professor of Cardiology, University of Amsterdam

Dr L. Koopmans
Director, TBI Holdings B.V., Rotterdam, and Professor of Health Sciences, University of Groningen

Dr F. van der Ploeg
Professor in Economics, University of Amsterdam

Dr D. Post
Professor of Social Medicine, University of Groningen; Medical Adviser of a Sickness Fund; member of the Christian Democratic Party

Professor Dr P.J. Vinken
Chairman, Management Council, Reed Elsevier PLC, Amsterdam

The committee was assisted by Dr E. Elsinga, Dr L.M.C. Ongering, Ms C.M. Visser (all employees of the Department of Health, Ministry of Health, Welfare and Sport).

COMMITTEE ON HEALTH DECISION-MAKING (WILLEMS COMMITTEE), 1993-4

Dr G. de Jong, Christian Democratic Party (CDA)

Dr A. de Jong, Social Democratic Party (PvdA)

Dr M.M.H. Kamp, Liberal Conservative Party (VVD)

Mr J. Kohnstamm, Liberal Democratic Party (D66) (Deputy Chairman)
Meindert Leerling, RPF (Confessional Party)

W.J. Willems, Green Left Party (Chairman)

Deputy-Members

Dr A. Lansink (CDA)

Ms T. Netelenbos (PvdA)

Mr J. van Rey (VVD)

Dr G. Ybema (D66)

Mr P. Rosenmöller (Green Left)

Engineer B.J. van der Vlies, SGP (Confessional Party)

COMMITTEE ON FUTURE FUNDING AND ORGANIZATION OF CARE FOR THE ELDERLY (WELSCHEN COMMITTEE)

Dr R.W. Welschen (Chairman)
Mayor

Dr H.J. Kaiser (Deputy Chairman)

Dr P.P.J. Houben
Professor of Economics

Dr C.A. de Kam, Social Democrat (PvdA)
Professor

Dr D. Post
Professor of Social Medicine, University of Groningen; medical advisor of a Sickness Fund; Christian Democratic Party (CDA)

Dr A.A. de Roo, Social Democrat (PvdA)
Professor of Economics

Dr F. Rutten
Professor of Economics, University of Rotterdam

Dr van der Schaar
Professor

Ms M.H.J. Jellesma-Eggenkamp
Geriatrician

The committee was assisted by Dr J. Bultman (Economic Advisor, Sickness Fund Council).

COMMITTEE ON SCALING UP PRIMARY EDUCATION (DE JAGER COMMITTEE), 1990

Mr De Jager (Chairman)
Education Department

Mr Holthuis (Deputy-Chairman)
Education Department

Dr N.A.J. Lagerweij
Professor, Utrecht University

Dr J.F.M. Claessen
Professor, Open University

Dr S. Boef-van der Meulen
Social and Cultural Planning Bureau

Dr H.M. Bronneman-Helmers
Social and Cultural Planning Bureau

Mr M.J. Keehnen
Education Department

Mr J.G. de Kok
Education Department

Dr G.J. Korevaar
Education Department

Mr F. Kraaijenbrink
Education Department

Dr M.E. Sandberg
Education Department

Dr H.W.M. Schoof
Education Department

Dr G.L.C. Vorstenbosch (Secretary)
Education Department

COMMITTEE ON THE EVALUATION OF PRIMARY EDUCATION (STEKENLENBURG COMMITTEE), 1991

Drs A.J.C. Stekelenburg, Chairman
Inspector-General, Department of Education

Dr B.M.P. Creemers
Professor, University of Groningen

Dr L. Eldering
Professor, University of Leiden

Dr A. van der Leij
Professor, Free University of Amsterdam

Dr van der Linden
Professor, University of Twente

Dr J. Sheerens
Professor, University of Twente

COMMITTEE ON PUPIL-BOUND FINANCE OF SPECIAL EDUCATION (RISPENS COMMITTEE), 1995

Dr J. Rispens (Chairman)
Professor of Orthopedagogy, University of Utrecht

Mr J. Wesemann
Advisor, Dutch Association of the Deaf

Mr P. Cremers
Independent Advisor

Dr B.P.M. Creemers
Professor of Pedagogy, University of Groningen

Mrs G.J. van der Lem
Director & Psychologist, Dutch Association for the Child that is Deaf or Hard of Hearing

Mr F.J.A. Razenberg
Director, Roman Catholic Primary School Sint Petrus, Boxtel

Mr P. Geelkerken
Deputy Head, Department of Education, Culture, Sports & Recreation, Association of Dutch Municipalities (VNG)

COMMITTEE ON QUALITATIVE ASPECTS OF FORM-SIZE IN PRIMARY EDUCATION (VAN EIJNDHOVEN COMMITTEE), 1996

Drs S.J.C. van Eijndhoven (Chairman)

Dr K.J. Polder (Secretary)
S.C.O. Kohnstamm Institute, University of Amsterdam

Mr D. van As
Head, Education Department, municipality of Haarlem

Dr R.J. Bosker
University teacher, Faculty of Applied Educational Science, Twente University

Mrs A.M. Joachim-Ruijs
Director, Christian Primary School 'de Loopplank', Zaandam

Dr A. Meijer
Refresher Course Co-ordinator, Catholic PABO, Zwolle, Interactum

Mrs A. Rotting-Braakman
Director, School for IOBK 'Het Bijvank', Enschede

EVALUATORY COMMITTEE 'TOGETHER IN SCHOOL AGAIN' (PESCHAR COMMITTEE), 1997

Dr J.L. Peschar (Chairman)
Professor of Sociology, University of Groningen

Dr C.J.W. Meijer (Coordinator)

W.W.P. van Wijngaarden (Secretary)

Independent Specialist-Committee Members

Professor L.M. Stevens

Professor G.W. Meijnen, University of Amsterdam

Professor J. Scheerens, Technical University, Twente

Professor K. Doornbos

Professor A. van der Leij

Dr I.W.T. Cuppens

Dr J. Kopmels

Representatives of Interest Groups

A. Board Organizations
- A. van Leijen, LVGS (National League of Calvinist School Associations)
- J.F. Voorthuizen, VGS
- Ms B.G. Havinga-Bakkes, PBCOI
- K.B.K. Hanslman, KBO League
- Mr S.J. Steen, VBS
- Drs A.F. Butenhuis, VNG

B. Personnel Organizations
- R. de Koning, ABOP

- J.H.A. Paulissen, NGL
- Ms M.E. Voorbij-van der Kooij, PCO
- E. Hasker, PCO
- Ms J.P.M. Roovers, CNV (education trade union)

C. Parent Organizations
- Dr M.S. Lok-Funcke, Parents & COO
- Dr Steffelaar-Moulijn, LOBO
- Dr A. Steen, LOBO
- E. Motelveld, VOO
- Ms C.M. van Jole-Royackers, MKO
- A.C. van Rooijen, NKO

D. National Process Management
- J. Vlaanderen ('Together to School Again')
- Dr J. Kok ('Primary Education')

E. National Pedagogic Centres
- Dr J. Kok
- Dr G.J. Makaske
- Dr J. Arts

F. Education Department
- Dr A.J.J. Dinglestad
- Dr A. Juli
- Dr R. Gonggrijp
- Dr P.J. Roemers

Appendix 2

Tables

TABLE I: ENROLMENT IN INDIA OF CHILDREN IN PRIMARY SCHOOL CLASSES I–IV

Year	*Gross enrolment ratio*	*Girls per 100 boys*
1951	42.6	39
1961	62.4	48
1971	76.4	60
1981	80.5	63
1991	101.0	71

SOURCE: P.N. Tyagi 1993, *Education for All*, New Delhi: National Institute of Educational Planning & Administration.

TABLE II: PUPIL-TEACHER RATIOS IN INDIA

Year	*Primary schools*	*Upper primary schools*
1951	24	20
1971	39	32
1991	43	37

SOURCE: *National Educational Survey*, New Delhi: NCERT, 1996.

TABLE III: SHARE OF CENTRE IN PLAN AND NON-PLAN EXPENDITURE ON EDUCATION IN INDIA

Year	*Plan expenditure*	*Non-plan expenditure*
1971–2	28.10	3.86
1981–2	24.64	4.50
1993–4	34.84	4.20

SOURCE: Government of India, 1995, *Budgetary Resources for Education 1951–52 to 1993–94*, New Delhi: Ministry of Human Resources Department.

TABLE IV: GOVERNMENT EXPENDITURE IN INDIA ON EDUCATION (PERCENTAGE OF TOTAL BUDGETS AT CENTRAL AND STATE LEVELS)

Year	*Central Budget*	*State Budgets*	*All-India total*
1951	1.01	14.75	7.92
1961	2.47	19.96	11.70
1971	1.46	20.31	9.53
1981	1.51	22.22	10.30
1991	2.74	21.78	12.58

SOURCE: Government of India, 1995, *Budgetary Resources for Education 1951–52 to 1993–94*, New Delhi: Ministry of Human Resources Department.

TABLE V: ESTIMATE OF ADDITIONAL RECURRENT COST OF UNIVERSAL PRIMARY EDUCATION: FIVE YEAR PLAN IN ACTION, INDIA

Year	*Primary school age population (million)*	*Children out of school each year to be provided (million)*	*Additoinal teachers required to reach 40:1 ratio (million)*	*Cost per year of education (million)*
1999	114.1	7.6	308	229
2000	115.5	16.7	308	500
2001	116.9	24.7	308	772
2002	118.3	34.8	308	1044
2003	119.8	43.9	308	1317

SOURCE: Haq and Haq (1998, p. 149).

Bibliography

Abraham, A.S., 1977, 'Medicare for the Villages: Why Second Rank Personnel are Needed', *Times of India*, 4 July, p. 8.

Alexander, P.C., 1991, *My Years with Mrs Gandhi,* New Delhi: Vision Books.

Alford, Robert A., 1972, 'The Political Economy of Health Care: Dynamics without Change', *Politics and Society*, vol. 12, pp. 127–64.

Allison, Graham, 1971, *The Essence of Decision*, Boston: Little, Brown.

Andeweg, R.B. and G.A. Irwin, 1993, *Dutch Government and Politics*, London: Macmillan.

Aquina, Herman and Hans Bekke, 1993. 'Governance in Interaction: Public Tasks and Private Organisations', in Jan Kooiman (ed.), *Modern Governance: New Government-Society Interactions*, London: Sage Publications, pp. 159–70.

Banerji, Debabar, 1993, 'Simplistic Approach to Health Policy Analysis: World Bank Teams on India Health Sector', *Economic and Political Weekly*, vol. 28, no. 24, pp. 1207–19.

BCVA (Bijzondere Commissie Vraagpunten Adviesorganen, 1993, *Raad op Maat* (*Measured Advice*), 's-Gravenhage: Kamer-stukken II, 1992–3, 21427, nos. 29 and 30.

Berman, Peter, 1998, 'Rethinking Health Care Systems: Private Health Care Provision in India', *World Development*, vol. 26, pp. 1463–79.

Berman, Peter and M.E. Khan (eds.), 1993, *Paying for India's Health Care*, New Delhi: Sage Publications.

Bhatt, Ramesh, 1993, 'The Private/Public Mix in Health Care in India', *Health Policy and Planning*, vol. 8, no. 1, pp. 43–56.

Bhore, Sir Joseph, 1946, *Report of the Health Survey and Development Committee*, New Delhi: Government of India.

Björkman, J.W., 1982, 'Professionalism in the Welfare State: Sociological Saviour or Political Pariah?' *European Journal of Political Research*, vol. 10, pp. 407–28.

———, 1993, 'The Mechanics of Professional Dominance in the Health Sector: Critical Clues from Comparative Perspective', in Benno Galjart and Patricio Silva (eds), *Designers of Development: Intellectuals and Technocrats in the Third World*, Leiden: Research School CNWS, pp. 153–65.

———, 2000, 'Pondering the Pedagogy of Public Policy Programs: Reflections on Curricular (Im)probabilities', *Africanus* (South Africa), vol. 30, no. 1, pp. 22–35.

———, 2001, 'Multiple Systems, Multiple Reforms: South Asian Health Policies in Comparative Perspective', in Stuart S. Nagel (ed.), *Handbook of Global Technology Policy*, New York: Marcel Dekker, Inc., pp. 167–220.

Björkman, J.W. and H.R. Chaturvedi, 1994, 'Panchayati Raj in Rajasthan: The Penalties of Success', in K. Schomer, J. Erdman, D. Lodrick and L. Rudolph (eds), *The Idea of Rajasthan: Explorations in Regional Identity* (2 vols), Delhi: Manohar, pp. 132–58.

Björkman, J.W. and K. Mathur, 1996, 'India: How a Government Party Decays When Government Swallows Party', in Jean Blondel and Maurizio Cotta (ed.), *Party and Government: An Inquiry into the Relationship between Governments and Supporting Parties in Western Liberal Democracies*, London: Macmillan, pp. 225–48.

Björkman, J.W. and K.G.H. Okma, 1997, 'Restructuring Health Care Systems in the Netherlands: The Institutional Heritage of Dutch Health Policy Reforms', in J.W. Björkman and C. Altenstetter, *Health Policy, National Schemes and Globalization*, London: Macmillan, pp. 79–108.

Björkman, J.W. and R.I. Schulz, 1981, 'On the Implementation of Change in National Health Delivery Systems: A Model and an Application', *Journal of Health and Human Resources Administration*, vol. 4, pp. 196–227.

Blanken, M., 1976, 'Force of Order and Methods', *An American View into the Dutch Directed Society*, The Hague: Martinus Nijhoff.

Brass, P., 1972, 'The Politics of Ayurvedic Education: A Case Study of Revivalism and Modernization in India', in Susanne Hoeber Rudolph and Lloyd I. Rudolph (eds), *Education and Politics in India*, Cambridge, Mass.: Harvard University Press, pp. 342–71, 452–9.

Caldwell, John C., P.H. Reddy and Pat Caldwell, 1984, 'The Determinants of Fertility Decline in Rural India', in T. Dyson and N. Crook (eds), *India's Demography: Essays on the Contemporary Population*, New Delhi: South Asia Publishers, pp. 187–207.

Caljé, K., 1992, 'Lubbers zet plan-Simons op sterk water tot 1 januari 1994', *NRC-Handelsblad*, Rotherdam, 10 April, p. 3.

Central Bureau of Health Intelligence, Government of India, 1993. *Health Information of India, 1992*, New Delhi: Ministry of Health and Family Welfare.

Chatterjee, Meera, 1988, *Implementing Health Policy*, Delhi: Manohar.

Chowdhury, N., 1983, 'Born to Die of Tetanus', *The Sunday Statesman* (New Delhi), 18 September, pp. 1, 7.

Das, S.K., 1998, *Civil Service Reform and Structural Adjustment*, Delhi: Oxford University Press.

De Swaan, A., 1989, *Zorg en de Staat* (*Care and the State: Health Care,*

Education and Welfare in Europe and the USA in the Modern Era), Amsterdam: Bert Bakker.

Djurfelt, Göran and Stefan Lindberg, 1975, *Pills against Poverty: A Study of the Introduction of Western Medicine in a Tamil Village*, Lund, Sweden: Scandinavian Institute of Asian Studies, Monograph Series No. 23.

Drèze, Jean and Amartya Sen, 1995, *India: Economic Development and Social Opportunity*, Delhi: Oxford University Press.

Duggal, Ravi, Sunil Nandraj and Sahana Shetty, 1992, *State Sector Health Expenditures Data Base: All India and State, 1951–85*, Bombay: Foundation for Research in Community Health.

The Economist, 22 February 1997.

Fortuyn, W.S.P., 1990, *Ordening door Ontvlechting* (*Order through De-Weaving*), Rijswijk: Ministery of Welfare, Health and Cultural Affairs.

Friedson, E., 1985, 'Reorganization of the Medical Profession', *Medical Care Review*, vol. 42, no. 11–35.

Galjart, Benno and Patricio Silva (eds), 1993, *Designers of Development: Intellectuals and Technocrats in the Third World*, Leiden: Research School CNWS.

van der Geest, S., J.D. Speckmann and P.H. Streefland, 1990, 'Primary Health Care in a Multi-level Perspective: Towards a Research Agenda', *Social Science and Medicine*, vol. 30, pp. 1025–34.

Gwatkin, D.R., S. Rutstein, K. Johnson, R.P. Pande and A. Wagstaff, 2000, *Socio-Economic Differences in Health, Nutrition, and Population in India*. Washington, DC: The World Bank.

Haq, M. and K. Haq, 1998, *Human Development in South Asia, 1998*, Karachi: Oxford University Press.

Heclo, Hugh, 1970, *Modern Social Policies in Britain and Sweden*, New Haven: Yale University Press.

Hindustan Times, 1984, '18,499 Medical Graduates Unemployed', New Delhi, 15 March, p. 8.

van der Hoeven, H.C., 1993, *Voor Elkaar: De Ziekenfondsen te Midden van Sociale Veranderingen* (*Serving Each Other: The Sickness Funds under Social Changes*), Utrecht: Centrale Bond van Onderling Beheerde Ziekenfondsen.

Holthoon, F.L., 1988, 'De Geschiedenis van het Publiek Domein in Nederland sinds 1815', in A.M.J. Kreukels and J.B.D. Simonis (eds), *Publiek Domein, De Veranderende Balans tussen Staat en Samenleving*, Meppel/Amsterdam: Boom.

ICSSR/ICMR (Indian Council of Social Science Research/Indian Council of Medical Research), 1981, *Health for All: An Alternative Strategy*, Pune: Indian Institute of Education.

Israel, J., 1998, *The Dutch Republic: Its Rise, Greatness, and Fall, 1477–1860*, Oxford: Clarendon Press.

Jeffrey, Roger, 1988, *The Politics of Health in India*, Berkeley: University of California Press.

Kakar, D.N., 1988, *Primary Health Care and Traditional Medical Practitioners*, New Delhi: Sterling Publishers.

Khilnani, Sunil, 1997, *The Idea of India*, London: Hamish Hamilton.

Kothari, Rajni, 1964, 'The Congress System in India'. *Asian Survey*, vol. 4 (12) pp. 1161–73.

———, 1970, *The Politics of India*, Boston: Little, Brown.

Lasswell, Harold D., 1951, 'The Policy Orientation', in Daniel Lerner and H.D. Lasswell (eds), *The Policy Sciences*, Palo Alto, California: Standford University Press, pp. 3–15.

Lijphart, Arend, 1968, *The Politics of Accommodation: Pluralism and Democracy in the Netherlands*, Berkeley: University of California Press.

———, 1984, *Democracies: Majoritarian and Consensus Patterns of Government in Twenty-One Countries*, New Haven: Yale University Press.

———, 1996, 'The Puzzle of Indian Democracy: A Consociational Interpretation', *American Political Science Review*, vol. 90 (2), pp. 258–68.

Lok Sabha Secretariat, 1985, *National Health Policy*, New Delhi: Government of India Press.

Manor, James, 1988, 'Parties and the Party System', in Atul Kohli (ed.), *India's Democracy*, Princeton: Princeton University Press, pp. 62–98.

Maru, Rishikesh M., 1983, 'The Community Health Volunteer Scheme in India: An Evaluation', *Social Science and Medicine*, vol. 17, pp. 1477–83.

Mathur, Kuldeep, 2001, 'Does Performance Matter? Policy Struggles in Education', *Journal of Educational Planning and Administration*, vol. 15 (2), pp. 225–40.

Mathur, Kuldeep, and J.W. Björkman, 1994, *Top Policy Makers in India*, New Delhi: Concept Publishers.

Ministry of Health and Family Welfare, 1980, *Curricula for Training of Staff of the Primary Health Centre*, New Delhi: Government of India.

———, 1981, *Report of the Working Group on 'Health for All by 2000 AD'*, New Delhi: Government of India.

———, 1982 through 1992 (various years), *Annual Report*, New Delhi: Government of India.

Morris-Jones, W.H., 1978, *Politics Mainly Indian*, Madras: Orient Longman.

Mosher, F., 1978, 'Professions in Public Service', *Public Administration Review*, vol. 38, pp. 144–50.

Naik, J.P., 1982, *The Education Commission and After*, New Delhi: Allied Publishers.

Nichter, Mark, 1980. 'Community Health Worker Scheme: A Plan for Democratisation', *Economic and Political Weekly*, vol. 15, no. 1, pp. 37–45.

Okma, G.H., 1997, *Studies on Dutch Health Politics, Policies and Law*, Utrecht: Ph.D. thesis, Medical Faculty.

Panikar, P.G.K., 1992, 'High Cost of Medical Care in Kerala: Tentative Hypothesis', *Economic and Political Weekly*, vol. 27, no. 23 pp. 1179–81.

Panikar, P.G.K., and C.R. Soman, 1984. *Health Status of Kerala: Paradox of Economic Backwardness and Health Development*, Trivandrum: Centre for Development Studies.

Plowden, William (ed.), 1987, *Advising the Rulers*, Oxford: Basil Blackwell.

Potter, David, 1996, *India's Political Administrators: From ICS to IAS*, Delhi: Oxford University Press.

Rajagopalan, S., 1984, '5000 Rural Docs Posts Vacant', *Hindustan Times*, (New Delhi) 5 January, pp. 1, 8.

Rogers, Everett M. and Douglas S. Solomon, 1975, *Traditional Midwives as Family Planning Communicators*, Honolulu: East–West Center.

Rudolph, Lloyd I. and Susanne Hoeber Rudolph, 1987, *In Pursuit of Lakshmi: The Political Economy of the Indian State*, Chicago: The University of Chicago Press.

van Schendelen, M.P.C.M., 1987, 'The Netherlands from High to Low Politicisation', in M.P.C.M. van Schendelen and R.J. Jackson (eds), *The Politicisation of Business in Western Europe*, London: Croom Helm.

Schnabel, P., 1988, 'De Gezondheidszorg: van Immuniteit tot Publiek Domein', in A.M.J. Kreukels and J.B.D. simonis (eds), *Publiek Domein, De Veranderende Balans tussen Staat en Samenleving*, Meppel/Amsterdam: Boom.

Schuler, P.J. Stannard and R. Warmenhoven, 1996, *The Education System of the Netherlands*, Den Haag: Netherlands University Foundation for International Cooperation (NUFFIC).

Srikantan, K. Sivaswamy, K. Balasubramanian and Surekha Nigam, 1984, 'The Performance of Family Planning Programme', in T. Dyson and N. Crook (eds), *India's Demography: Essays on the Contemporary Population*, New Delhi: South Asia Publishers, pp. 159–74.

Subramaniam, Jeane, 1995, 'A Stitch in Time'. *Business India*, 27 March–9 April, p. 195.

Tulasidhar, V.B., 1996, *Public Financing for Health in India: Recent Trends*, Washington, DC: International Health Policy Program.

Udupa, K.N. 1975, 'The Ayurvedic System of Medicine in India', in Kenneth W. Newell (ed.), *Health by the People*, Geneva: World Health Organization.

United Nations Development Program (UNDP), 1996, *Human Development Report 1996*, New York: Oxford University Press.

Varma, P.K., 1998, *The Great Indian Middle Class*, New Delhi: Viking Penguin Press.

Weiner, Myron, 1967, *Party Building in a New Nation*, Chicago: University of Chicago Press.

Wheare, Kenneth C., 1955, *Government by Committee: An Essay on the British Constitution*, Oxford: Clarendon Press.

World Bank, 1993, *World Development Report 1993: Investing in Health*, New York: Oxford University Press.

———, 1998, *Reducing Poverty in India: Options for More Effective Public Services*, Washington, DC: The World Bank.

Yadav, Yogender, 1999, 'Electoral Politics in the Time of Change: India's Third Electoral System, 1989–99', *Economic and Political Weekly*, vol. 34, nos. 34 and 35, pp. 2393–9.

Index